ILLUMINATIONS

THE UFO EXPERIENCE AS
A PARAPSYCHOLOGICAL EVENT

ERIC OUELLET, PH.D.

ANOMALIST BOOKS
*San Antonio * Charlottesville*

An Original Publication of Anomalist Books

**Illuminations: The UFO Experience as a
Parapsychological Event**
Copyright © 2015 Eric Ouellet
ISBN: 978-1-938398-53-7
Second Edition

Cover photo © Maxiphoto/iStock

Book design by Seale Studios

For information, go to AnomalistBooks.com, or write to:
Anomalist Books,
5150 Broadway #108,
San Antonio, TX 78209

Contents

Foreword

A few years ago a woman reported to me that she had seen an unidentified flying object. She was one of thousands to do so since the 1970s and had joined millions of others from almost every country on Earth to share in this unexpected adventure.

It is likely many readers of this book have either personally seen something in the sky which they cannot explain or know someone who claims to have done so. This is not a rare event at all. So that there is some kind of UFO phenomenon in need of resolution is not in question. But still very much open to discussion is what *causes* these UFOs to appear in the first place.

My witness—Jenny, as it happens—had a particularly intense experience near her home in the Pennine Hills of England. She relived it as we walked the route of her close encounter down the steep slopes above Walsden village in Yorkshire. Locals call this area "UFO alley" because it is has been home to so many sightings for a century.

Jenny was no wide eyed believer in little green men. Indeed, few witnesses fit with that stereotype and come from just about every part of the human spectrum in terms of occupation and opinion on the subject. She was in fact a care worker in a children's home, used to dealing with all sorts of human drama whilst adopting a patient resolve. Yet this composure could not prepare the clearly bemused woman talking to me for what took place on that ordinary fall day back in 1978.

Relaxing after work Jenny had ridden her horse at a moor top stables and at about 6:30 PM was heading home in gathering gloom along with her Whippet dog, which was actively sniffing the twisting path as they descended steeply towards the village below.

"Suddenly," she told me, "for the first and only time ever, my dog slid to a halt in the midst of his frolicking and stared up into the sky. Had he not done this I would never have looked up myself and just walked on by right underneath. But he knew something was up there. And it was."

As she stared skyward, she did a double take, looked back at the star struck animal, shook her head and returned to the object. It was still there. A neon blue lens shape with what looked like three round yellowish holes or windows in a band across the middle. Surrounding it was a "weird greenish silver cloud which thinned towards its edges." Like a fuzzy aura encompassing the UFO.

Jenny was now just as transfixed as her pet. In fact she struggled visibly in the interview to find words to describe the emotional impact of this encounter. She tried several metaphors to relate the sudden jolt to her being before settling on one.

"If you were to take a walk over the moors and the QE 2 [the ocean liner *Queen Elizabeth 2*] suddenly materialised in front of you then you'd feel what I felt. Knowing it had happened but realising at the same time that it was impossible and you could not believe what you were seeing and so could never try to tell others to do so."

Up until that moment, Jenny argued, she believed that as a no nonsense woman then she would just tell everyone openly if she saw something in the sky and tell them that it was all real. But the sheer emotional impact and implausibility of what she had witnessed that evening made all surety evaporate amidst what was an intensely personal experience.

Whilst looking upward Jenny felt an awe that bordered on a religious experience with a set of feelings that I have heard often described to me in such cases. They seem to act like a doorway between our reality and a different level altogether—as if passing into a magical realm where the everyday world is replaced by something far outside our normal view of the universe. In a flash not only has everything you believed to be true changed but so has your entire grasp of the very meaning of the universe. Normal life has imploded around you like a star going nova.

Amongst this set of symptoms reported by Jenny and others is an electrical tingling that vibrates through the body, a sense of how the passage of time loses meaning and an isolation that encases the witness in a bubble of reality that cuts them off from the old world.

Jenny told me that there was a kind of aura emitted by the UFO that seeped out *"everything else from my consciousness."* She used an apt phrase to describe her bond with the UFO—*"being joined at the soul."* Given her dog seemingly was also "locked on" to the object then perhaps even her pet was emotionally bonded to this bizarre phenomenon.

She added with shock: "I swear that had something got out of the thing and said 'come with me' then I would have followed like a lamb."

Jenny now "felt" rather than "heard" a voice that was "tickling" inside of her mind, repeating over and over one phrase — "do not be afraid." Only later did she realise that this was like her own "thinking voice" and not someone talking to her yet she believed what it told her implicitly.

So was this just a visionary experience as such things suggest? Nobody else in the valley reported this spectacle. Yet how could it be personalised if her dog saw it too and even before she did? It was as if a "Sphere of Influence" surrounded this UFO encounter. Outside of here you might see nothing extraordinary, or perhaps just a distant light in the sky. You had to be inside the boundaries of this sphere to undergo a full blown close encounter.

Case after case has been followed up by my research and fitted this pattern persuading me that this must be a clue about the nature of the UFO phenomenon.

Two years later, almost to the day, a police officer called Alan Godfrey, who during the 1980s was the local village cop for Walsden, underwent a close encounter under two miles away in Todmorden in what became one of the most famous "alien abductions" in Britain, and I have investigated dozens of other cases from this same small area now. Something unusual is going on.

Are certain locations, such as this valley, haunted by UFOs? Perhaps, but there also remains another vital component to every sighting—the witness themselves. Should we investigate *them* just as much as we investigate the UFOs that they see?

Jenny instinctively "knew" that her UFO was about to disappear. A wave of desolation soaked into her consciousness and she began pleading vocally for it to stay. But instead it split into two parts that zapped apart like stones from a catapult zooming off in different directions. A shower of electric sparks trailed in their wake as they vanished over the horizon.

On the hillside, Jenny collapsed onto the ground openly sobbing, and it was some time before her composure returned enough to soothe her exhausted dog and continue their slow walk homeward. After finding one of my books in the library, Jenny eventually decided that I might listen to her story without judging her sanity.

By then I had been putting the pieces of the UFO puzzle together for many years and knew that cases such as hers appeared pivotal to our understanding of what seems to be going on. Whatever the ultimate explanation proves to be, it is far more complex than so often judged by commentators on this mystery.

It behaves like something that is closer to the realms of inner space than the vast reaches of outer space.

From experience I knew to ask the sort of questions of Jenny that UFO researchers rarely consider relevant and got the kind of answers that I find are remarkably common. They involve areas of human experience that might seem to have little relation to seeing strange object in the sky.

Jenny's life was a catalogue of extraordinary events that I have come across again and again. Out of body experiences, lucid dreams, precognitions, time lapses, and many other things have occurred throughout her life and place her close encounter into a broader context that seems much more interesting. If you choose to ignore these other things then you reject half the story that surely describes how and why that UFO appeared over those moors back in 1978.

But what are we then to make of another oddity—Jenny's unusual level of early life recall? Most of us cannot describe events that occurred before about the age of three because of changes in how the brain records and stores memories whilst young children develop. Jenny *could* recall them—and I have found so can lots of other witnesses to UFO close encounters.

Moreover, she, again like many such witnesses (including that police officer abducted in the same valley), described odd things that happened when a young child in her bedroom. Jenny and these other witnesses report small balls of light that appear near to their crib and float around the bedroom, as if teasing them to reach out and grab hold. I call them "Psychic Toys" because they crop up so often that I think they may be a pointer to the bigger picture. I wonder if they introduce the child to the ability to handle psychic events—almost as if training them to handle such aspects of their brain much like normal toys assist a child to adapt motor skills and other mundane abilities.

Jenny also had a vivid creative imagination just like so many others that I have come across in UFO cases. They write songs or poems or paint skilfully. Their artistic prowess seems well above the normal level and this appears unlikely to be yet another coincidence.

For me these are signposts that guide us in unexpected directions towards a possible answer to the UFO riddle. But how do you put such things together into a cohesive explanation?

Happily, that is precisely where this book comes in. As a sociologist and a UFO witness, plus, importantly, a parapsychological researcher, Eric Ouellet ticks all the boxes to appreciate the bagatelle of curiosities that I have encountered in the field during 40 years of UFO investigation.

He has reached his conclusions in an interesting way. So I am very pleased that, unlike so many UFO researchers, he has not run from the consequences that these uncomfortable ideas bring to any past assumptions. Instead he has embraced them as steps to lead us forward—which they are.

Eric has pieced his own set of clues together and started to ask the right kind of questions that seem to be leading him towards a theory of explanation that just might work. To get there, he asks the reader only to lay aside prior expectations about what you assume causes UFO sightings.

So sit back and let the author tell you his own story, as he does quite eloquently. Let him then be your guide as he sketches out a route through the maze of evidence that he unravels on a route to unexpected conclusions.

Whether in the end you share his confidence as to the direction that he seems to be headed, his suggestions are well in line with the UFO mystery as I have come to know it over the years.

UFOs are not straightforward and they are not obviously resolved as one simple thing or another—whatever you may have read or seen on TV documentaries up to now. They might require a complete revolution in your thinking if you really want to find some answers.

This book does all of that and will open your eyes to a novel way of contemplating the evidence. I hope and expect it will be just the start of a debate urging a different approach towards unravelling the truth.

Jenny Randles
Cheshire, England
August 2015

Introduction

Thousands if not millions of people have observed what are generally called UFOs over the last one hundred years. Many cases have been well researched by the military and intelligence services as well as by scientists and private individuals. Yet we are no closer today to knowing what UFOs are than we were a century ago.

Over time various explanations and hypotheses have been put forward to make sense of the UFO enigma. One particular explanation became better known and remains the most popular and conventional one among those interested in the UFO enigma: UFOs as spaceships coming from another planet and piloted by extraterrestrial beings. This view is called the Extra-Terrestrial Hypothesis (ETH). Others have proposed somewhat different origins for UFOs: they are interdimensional visitors or time travelers. And while most UFO researchers concede that the vast majority of UFO sightings are simply mistaken perceptions, such as planes, helicopters, satellites, weather balloons, Chinese lanterns, hoaxes, collective hallucinations, and delusions, a hardcover group of skeptics contend that *all* UFO events are misperceptions. So since the early days of the modern UFO phenomenon (since the well-publicized sighting by Kenneth Arnold in June 1947) we have been stuck between two untenable alternatives: they are either aliens from another planet (or dimension), or they are all misperceptions. Consequently we have made very little progress in explaining the origin of UFOs. But are we really stuck because of the nature of the evidence at hand?

No.

The enigma persists mostly because of another problem. Only a few of those who are seriously studying UFOs are willing to look at alternative approaches. This problem was recognized many years ago, and it is still an ongoing issue.[1] As the famous quote attributed to Einstein says: "Insanity is doing the same thing over and over again and expecting different results." This applies very well to the current world of UFO research.

It is time to try something new.

This book proposes a way out of this situation; one that may eventually lead to a better understanding of the phenomenon. It proposes that UFOs are parapsychological phenomena. Those who are well versed in the UFO literature may object that the "paranormal hypothesis," namely that UFOs are something more akin to ghosts than alien visitors, has been considered and rejected. But the parapsychological approach I present in this book is not based on the actions of ethereal or trans-dimensional entities of any kind. It implies, instead, a form of human potential that is not well understood. This is the working assumption of this book. To be clear, it is not stated here as a proven reality, but rather it is the starting point of a hypothesis designed to approach the UFO phenomenon from a different angle. I call this approach the parapsychological hypothesis because it is essentially based on ideas, knowledge, models, and findings that are found in the field of scientific parapsychology.

The parapsychological approach, however, is not enough in itself to get "unstuck;" we also need a different appreciation of the evidence at hand. The UFO phenomenon appears to be a mixture of poorly understood forces, playing on different levels. On one level, it can be very personal, and at times it is a troubling or even life-changing experience for the witness. Many reports of close encounters with what was construed as non-human entities attest to that. On another level, it also exhibits patterns and commonalities that are impersonal and appear completely disconnected from the witnesses. Similarities in strange and odd flying patterns and shapes reported by multiple witnesses clearly illustrate this aspect of the UFO phenomenon.

This double dynamic of the personal and the impersonal is probably the most confusing characteristic of the UFO experience. How can something be both deeply personal and impersonal at the same time, especially when the two do not seem to match? People have often tried to connect these two apparently contradictory dynamics, the personal and the impersonal (or collective), by assigning a metaphysical meaning to the experience. An extraordinary personal experience with a strange light becomes also an encounter with strange beings sharing higher knowledge about the Universe; other witnesses in a different location just saw the "machine" used by the strange beings. In a different age these beings would have been called angels or fairies; today they are called aliens. The personal experience becomes part of a larger narrative, and hence a direct connection is established between the personal experience and the seemly impersonal occurrence.

When the personal and the impersonal are too divergent, there is a tendency to object, saying that only one level can be true. In other words, either people having a very weird personal close encounter are hallucinating because other "objective" witnesses cannot corroborate the events, or the close encounter was the real deal because it "fits" what others have reported before. Take for instance a case I investigated in 2014. A lady claimed to have seen a strange smoky green orb moving towards her while she was alone at home a number of years ago. She felt paralyzed and could not do anything until it left. She had a number of odd and strange experiences in her life that involved UFO sightings and paranormal events, both before and after this particular incident. For her, it was obvious that the green ball she witnessed was a manifestation of some sort of alien entity. She made a connection between her other experiences and that specific one. Yet most ufologists would dismiss her experience as something other than a UFO experience, that she was maybe dreaming perhaps, and that in any event this does not "fit" the pattern of close encounters as there were no humanoid entities involved. The meanings and the words we use to describe strange things tend to limit our understanding of the complex reality of UFOs.

So this book not only proposes a parapsychological approach to the UFO phenomenon, but it also offers a perspective that maintains as real both levels of the experience; this is not a matter of either/or. The apparent disconnect between deeply personal experiences and larger impersonal events may be so only because of how we look at things. By changing how we look at the evidence, we can see new possibilities. To go back to this 2014 case, one can say that the lady had a paranormal experience. But later on she also had a UFO sighting involving another witness. The personal and the impersonal can co-exist; they do not need to be artificially "boxed" in arbitrary assumptions.

At a more conceptual level, the mathematical concept of fractals can help us understand how a model can incorporate the personal and impersonal aspects of the UFO experience. One way to look at fractals is to imagine a large triangle made of smaller triangles, which are themselves made of yet another set of smaller triangles. They are all triangles, but they cannot be reduced to one another; they co-exist on their own respective level of reality. The bigger triangle exists independently of the others but it needs the smaller ones to exist; at the same time the smaller ones are part of the bigger one, but they can be seen as triangles on their own without referring to the bigger one. These triangles co-exist independently, but are part of the whole.

Sierpinski triangle, an example of fractal configuration[2]

This generic way of looking at inter-relationships between levels of reality, while respecting their individual characteristics, applies to the UFO experience as well. For instance, the lady from the example given above could be construed as psychically sensitive and thus having a lot personal experiences, while also being sensitive to other impersonal paranormal forces. In this particular case, sensitivity to psychical events might be the common thread, not the actual content or the origins of the experience.

My high school teachers were not aliens
My motivation to write this book goes back to my younger years. In the summer of 1974 or 1975, when I was a kid, a set of strange lights appeared in the night sky of Quebec City, Canada. My two older teenage brothers noticed it first through a window in our house, on the upper floor. They were very agitated, but one of them had the presence of mind to get our father's binoculars. They took turns looking at the lights with the binoculars. They took their time; at least it seemed like an eternity for me. After bugging them repeatedly, they finally allowed me to use the binoculars. But no matter how hard I looked, I could not find the lights. At that point, they ran downstairs to get our parents, and when the rest of the family finally arrived upstairs, there was nothing to see. I asked my brothers what they saw, and they described it as a group of yellow-orange lights in a circle, a bit like a circle of bulbs on a flat chandelier. I was not a UFO witness, but I was a witness to a UFO observation. It became obvious to me that to understand UFOs, one has to understand people. My interest in the topic remained latent until I met a friend who was very much interested in UFOs during my doctoral studies in the mid-1990s. I started to read avidly the literature on the topic.

The more I read, however, the more I became disappointed with what I found. Most of the older books on the topic were just a series of short descriptive stories of UFO observations, offering little analysis to make sense of the phenomenon. The more recent ones (in those days) were almost all about conspiracy theories regarding governments hiding information about UFOs or they made absolutely outlandish and unsubstantiated claims about the UFOs themselves. In fact, in my view, there was a sort of competition among writers as to who would make the craziest claim about governmental knowledge on UFOs, especially in the United States. Even worse, my Master's degree was in the field of Government Studies and Public Administration, and I was doing my Ph.D. in Organizational Sociology at the time. I could see how those writers had not the slightest clue how bureaucracies work; they would take the most insignificant detail of a declassified report and make it say just about anything they wanted. This was not the finest hour for the field of UFOlogy.

I eventually focused on the UFO literature produced by the few who were offering some serious thinking about the phenomenon, most of which was written between the late 1960s and the mid-1980s. Much of this material dealt with the paranormal dimension of the UFO phenomenon. Even the CIA, according to its official historian, briefly looked into UFOs from a paranormal and parapsychological perspective in the late 1970s and early 1980s, before giving up on the topic.[3] One thing that became clear to me is that serious research on UFOs did occur, and it had a common theme. Hence, the approach taken for this book is not arbitrary; it attempts to pick up where the study of UFOs as a paranormal phenomenon left off more than 25 years ago.

After finally graduating with a Ph.D., I decided to approach the UFO phenomenon like any other academic research project, that is by doing a review of the analytical literature looking for what is known, what is plausible, where the gaps in our knowledge lay, etc. In 2005, I started to put down my ideas in writing in a blog in French, my native language. As most of the literature on the topic is in English, I decided to start a new blog in 2008 under the name Parasociology. I started to gather more documents, and as my ideas were starting to become clearer I decided that it was time to put them into a comprehensive book.

Interestingly, it was only in February 2010 that I actually had a UFO experience. During a cold night in a northern suburb of Toronto, Canada, I was waiting in the warmth of my car for my kids to come out of a store. I saw a stationary light in the night sky, a bit brighter than the other stars. At first I thought it was

Venus. But for some reason my attention kept going back to that light. After observing it for two or three minutes, the light started to move and it zipped away towards the west, disappearing over the horizon in about two seconds. This could not be a meteorite or shooting star, as they cannot remain stationary. It could not be a plane, helicopter, missile, or satellite, as they cannot accelerate that fast. As far as I know, I was not hallucinating or delusional. Yet, it was just a light in the night sky, and as far as I can tell this observation remains unexplainable. The truly fascinating aspect of this experience for me was not so much the extreme acceleration of the light, but the strange feeling of attraction I felt towards it when it was stationary.

I was never visited by Men-in-Black
I am a civilian working for a military organization, and, yes, I have a high-level security clearance. Some people prone to conspiracy theories might think that this book is just part of the "cover-up" about UFOs, because it does not feed into the extraterrestrial hypothesis or into conspiracy theory. These people can think whatever they want. This book is not addressed to them. For those who keep an open mind about the UFO phenomenon, let me state a few things for the record.

In spite of my own investigations, I have not seen anything in the military world about UFOs. Some people in uniform are open-minded about it. A few have seen a UFO. Others laugh at it or smile when talking about it. The vast majority, however, are just indifferent to the issue. This is the reality of UFOs in the military today. For those truly interested in the military and intelligence communities interest in the UFO phenomenon, I strongly recommend John Alexander's book *UFOs: Myths, Conspiracies, and Realities,* published in 2012. Alexander provides a substantive look and analysis about the way military and intelligence-related bureaucracies work, and how they have handled the UFO issue over the years, particularly in the United States. Those organizations did not always deal with the topic in the most honest way, especially from the 1950s until the mid-1980s. But in the end, they do not have much knowledge about

UFOs. UFOs are met with a great deal of institutional indifference in the military in the 21st century; it is not the big "hush-hush" topic that some popular writers would like us to believe.

The second point I would like to emphasize is that I am not a member of any UFO research organization, although I was member of MUFON for one year in the mid-2000s. My views are not representative of any particular UFO group either. I have attended meetings of some UFO research organizations over the years, where I've encountered many people unwilling to consider any new idea.

I am a professional member of the Parapsychological Association (PA), but I am not representing their informal views either. The UFO subject remains contentious among the members of the PA. This organization was created to provide a forum and legitimacy to those who engage in scholarly and scientific research on paranormal phenomena. Given that UFOlogy has been plagued by a lot of nonsense, outlandish claims, and very doctrinaire attitudes towards any explanations not based on the ETH, the PA members' attitude is quite understandable. Although the idea that UFOs could be a form of paranormal phenomenon is not entirely new, the PA states on its official website that it does not study UFOs.

The need for a greater degree of open-mindedness about the UFO phenomenon can be seen everywhere.

SECTION ONE
Studying UFOs

Chapter 1
What Is Known About UFOs

On March 21, 2004, just before 8:00 PM, the pilot of a private jet carrying the Prime Minister of Canada, Paul Martin, reported seeing a bright, unidentified object while flying over Alberta. A few days later, many thought the object had likely been a meteor. Yet less than one week later, on March 27, around 8:30 PM, two witnesses noted a big luminous ball in the sky, near Rigaud in Quebec between Ottawa and Montreal. Then at 10:45 PM, a witness noted two red balls of light flying together in the sky over Montreal. On March 28 at 2:25 AM a witness in Prince George, British Columbia, saw two orange balls of light flying until one of them separated and disappeared over the horizon; the second one also disappeared not long after. At around 5:10 PM that same day three witnesses saw two metallic colored flying discs while playing golf near Calgary, Alberta, moving very fast across the sky. Finally, around 9:45 PM, three Canadian Government employees who were in the air traffic control tower of a major Canadian airport noticed an unusual bright red light moving over the horizon for about 30 seconds. They estimated that it was between 5 and 8 miles from them. There was no radar or transponder return and it left no trail behind. After checking with a nearby military base, they confirmed there were no military flights at the time either. No other witnesses seemed to have noticed the light. Interestingly, the light followed the same apparent track as a Boeing 737 that arrived about 30 minutes later.[4]

This story of UFO sightings is interesting in many regards. It could be considered a mini UFO wave. Similar, but not necessarily identical, objects were observed pretty much at both ends of the North American continent. It involved a well-known high-level politician, multiple witnesses, multiple objects, strange flying behaviors, as well as uncertainty about whether the sightings were actually unidentified. And with the final sighting a potential premonition or at least some sort of symbolic synchronicity seemed to be involved. Cases like this one can be quite fascinating, but they are usually too short on information to be conclusive. What if some sort of premonition was involved; was it about the Boeing 737 itself or about someone onboard? Would another plane, flying later on, but on the same flight path have had the same significance? Was there some sort of common pattern among the witnesses? We do not know, and it is likely we will never know.

This is a very common problem in the study of UFOs. Most UFO reports are only available if someone voluntarily contacts some UFO organization. These UFO organizations are run by volunteers who have limited resources for conducting any sort of substantive investigation. Most of these volunteers also tend to be interested in proving the extraterrestrial hypothesis (ETH) and to focus only on elements that fit the ETH, paying at best only scant attention to other aspects of the case. But even more problematic, the witness himself or herself usually pays attention only to a few elements of the sighting, and not necessarily the ones that might provide the most useful information. The net result is that although there might be tens of thousands of UFO reports out there, only a few are amenable to sound analysis. This problem was highlighted by newsman and UFO investigator John Keel over 25 years ago.[5] With the gradual decline of so many UFO research organizations in the last 15 years, this problem is even more acute now than ever.

As one can see, the study of UFOs is not a simple task, and it definitely requires going far beyond the description of the object seen and writing a UFO report about it. The good news is that a number of researchers have gone the extra mile and produced some interesting findings about UFOs. Those findings, however, may be surprising to those not familiar with UFO research literature that simply describes UFO events.

Studying UFOs: the basics
The term "Unidentified Flying Object" (UFO) was developed by the U.S. Air Force in the early 1950s to describe, in a generic manner, "any object which by performance, aerodynamic characteristics, or unusual feature does not conform to any

presently known aircraft or missile type, or which cannot be positively identified as a familiar object."[6] Later, the term UFO was favored to replace the then more popular notion of "flying saucer," which was perceived as too narrow and biased towards a particular view of the phenomenon, as not all UFOs were described to be in the shape of a saucer. But from the onset, whether one was using the expression "flying saucers" or "UFO," those strange events in the sky were implicitly assumed to be caused by physical objects. In the end, the key difference was whether one believed these objects were of human, natural, or extraterrestrial (sentient) origin.

This assumption that UFOs are "objects" is just that: an assumption. The emphasis placed by the U.S. Air Force on "flying objects" was quite understandable in the context of the Cold War, as worry spread that the Soviet Union would develop new types of high performance aircraft or missile to threaten the United States and the free world. Similarly, in the early days of the space age, naïve belief about space travel was understandable; it was not irrational to think that flying saucers were spaceships controlled by extraterrestrial visitors. It is in this context that a curious consensus emerged in the selection of the term UFO to describe something of an assumed material nature. Whether one believed that UFOs were misperceived weather balloons, aircrafts, missiles, meteors, planets and stars, or spaceships from another world, they all believed that something physical, or material, was seen. This materialistic view, however, is rather simplistic. Nowadays, some researchers prefer to use the expression UAP, for Unexplained Aerial Phenomenon, as the term UFO implies that there is an "object" present. For similar reasons, some governmental agencies prefer to use the acronym UAS for Unidentified Aerial Sighting.

Modern UFOlogy, since its "official" beginning in June 1947 with the highly publicized UFO sighting by Kenneth Arnold near Mount Rainier in Washington State, has excluded many important possibilities about what UFOs could be. Within days of Arnold's sighting some newspaper reporters hypothesized that UFOs could be spaceships coming from another planet, although most still thought they were either a Soviet aircraft or some sort of unusual natural phenomenon. Yet, very early in the history of UFO research, serious doubts were raised about the possibility that UFOs could be spaceships. One of the earliest doubters is on display in a 1948 report commissioned by the U.S. Air Force, analyzing the possibility that UFOs could be of extraterrestrial origin. The author of the report, J. E. Lipp, was quite clear in concluding that "[a]lthough visits from outer space are believed to be possible, they are believed to be very improbable. In particular, the actions reported to the 'flying objects' reported during 1947 and 1948 seem inconsistent with the requirements for space travel."[7] This was a conclusion based on what is known about physics. What is more interesting is that the report went beyond determining if there were "flying objects" or not, and incorporated in the analysis the so-called subjective dimension. Lipp was quite insightful about the rather "human" nature of UFOs when he wrote that: "The distribution of flying objects is peculiar, to say the least. As far as this writer knows, all incidents have occurred within the United States, whereas visiting spacemen could be expected to scatter their visits more or less uniformly over the globe. The small area covered indicates strongly that the flying objects are of Earthly origin, whether physical or psychological."[8]

Just one year after the Kenneth Arnold incident, Lipp was able to put his finger on a key issue. UFOs were probably a mixture of physical and psychological phenomena. The Lipp report was only made public many years later, but the data used for the analysis was for the most part public. The elusive character of UFOs is certainly the most important material characteristic of this phenomenon. Although UFOs are sometimes said to leave traces, no conclusive physical evidence is ever found. In fact, even before 1947, the U.S. military was confronted with a strange phenomenon that was not fully physical, so to speak.

On Thursday October 14, 1943, a group of over 300 U.S. Army Air Force B-17s were flying on a day bombing mission over Schweinfurt, Germany. During this mission, the American strategic bombing forces had one of their worst missions of the war, with only 197 aircraft returning, many of which were seriously damaged. This day became known in USAF annals as the Black Thursday. Just before this tragic event of the Second World War, something very unusual happened. Here is the content of the official report:[9]

EKG.　　TELEGRAM EN CLAIR　　4112
Recd. AMCS. 171129a hrs Oct.43
To- OIAWW, OIAJX, OISHL, HBC, AMY.

From - OIPNT

IMPORTANT. CONFIDENTIAL.

8 BC 0-1079-E
Annex to Intelligence Report Mission Schweinfurt 16 October 1943

306 Group report a partially unexploded 20mm shell imbedded above the panel in the cockpit of A/C [Aircraft] number 412 bearing the following figures 19K43. The Group Ordnance Officer believes the steel composing the shell is of inferior grade. 348th Group reports a cluster of disks observed in the path of the formation near Schweinfurt, at the time there were no E/A [enemy aircraft] above. Discs were described as silver coloured — one inch thick and three inches in diameter. They were gliding slowly down in very uniform cluster. A/C 026 was unable to avoid them and his right wing went directly through a cluster with absolutely no effect on engines or plane surface. One of the discs was heard striking tail assembly but no explosion was observed. About 20 feet from these discs a mass of black debris of varying sizes in clusters of 3 by 4 feet. Also observed 2 other A/C flying through silver discs with no apparent damage. Observed discs and debris 2 other times but could not determine where it came from.

Copies to:-
P.R. & A.I.6.
D.B.Ops
War Room
D.A.T.
A.I.3. (USA) (Action 2 copies)

What is fascinating about this early flying disc report is that it was not only observed by multiple aircrafts from different angles, but it also came into physical contact with the aircraft without causing any damage, as if it was only partially physical. And even more important, this UFO incident happened just before a terrible tragedy befell these American airmen. Was this incident also a sort of externalized premonition of what was coming, one that was not understood by anyone? UFO events seem to be more complicated that just "crafts" flying around.

What do we know about the physical aspects of UFOs?

As already noted, no UFO-related physical material has ever been found that could withstand objective and transparent scientific study. By the 1960s, this lack of physical evidence began to shake the core assumptions held by various ufologists. It was in this context, for example, that astronomer J. Allen Hynek, one of the pioneers of modern UFOlogy, became disappointed with the ETH, according to a 1970s interview; it was then that he decided to explore other hypotheses that could take into account the fundamentally elusive character of UFOs.[10]

As various researchers were trying to understand the physical dimension of the UFO phenomenon, one particular recurrent theme started to emerge: UFOs tend to have electromagnetic properties. The key words here are "tend to," namely it is a characteristics that is frequent, but not necessarily demonstrable in every UFO sighting. However, without precluding any possible future findings about the physical dimension of the UFO phenomenon, electromagnetism remains the most common denominator for the time being.

One of the first serious proposals, which emerged in the 1960s, about the physical nature of UFO was that they were ball lightning caused by unusual weather electrical conditions. Unfortunately, this idea was pushed a bit too zealously by some UFO "debunkers" and came to be ignored by the UFO community. Now, as time has passed, this notion that *some* UFOs could be caused by ball lightning is being seriously considered by researchers whose work has appeared in various scientific journals in physics and meteorology, among others.[11] This phenomenon is still not well understood, especially concerning the necessary conditions for the appearance of ball lightning and why some last much longer than others.

The electromagnetic properties of UFOs have been linked to a similar but different natural phenomenon: balls of plasma, better known as earthlights. Earthlights are essentially highly heated, highly charged gas bubbles that escape from the Earth's crust. It is an exotic phenomenon and we still do not know much about it. At night they appear as either fast moving or stationary lights in the sky, while during the day they look like spherical or saucer-shaped silvery objects. From a visual standpoint, their similarity to many UFO sightings is striking.

Some who are well acquainted with the UFO literature might argue that not all UFO sightings can be described as earthlights, or some other forms of balls of plasma. Many witnesses over the years have described objects that have the shape of a manufactured object, like a triangle. This assessment is correct. However, in terms of known physical properties, we do not know anything about any potential manufactured objects, while there is some knowledge about the role of earthlights in the UFO phenomenon. Furthermore, electromagnetism also interacts with the human mind in certain conditions, and this warrants paying a closer attention to it even if it does not explain every single UFO observation.

The notion that earthlights may have something to do with the UFO phenomenon is not new. In 1968, John Keel[12] and French researcher Ferdinand Lagarde[13] independently noted that UFO sightings tend to be over-represented in areas where there are known geological faults and geomagnetic anomalies. This finding actually confirmed what Charles Fort[14] had found earlier;

he had noted that there was a strong correlation between the observation of earthlights and earthquakes, which are known to occur more frequently where there are geological faults. Lagarde wrote a book[15] on the topic a few years later. A research project was eventually established in the 1980s at Hessdalen in Norway, an area well known for regularly producing earthlights.[16] The research remains ongoing and much remains to be understood about this phenomenon. Its energy source remains poorly understood, but it is now proven that they can be detected by radars while not being visible to the naked eye.[17]

Another interesting study was conducted by Jacques Vallée during the 1970s. He performed a computerized content analysis of a large number of UFO sighting reports and the only thing in common that he found was that such events started by the perception of a light in the sky or on the ground.[18] This finding added weight to link earthlights and UFOs, as it was consistent with what witnesses were reporting in UFO sightings. Also during the 1970s, some researchers remarked that solar activity might also be playing a role in producing UFO sightings. Using an extensive data set provided by Allen Hynek, the Swedish researcher Forshufvud[19] noted a significant correlation between UFO sightings and solar activity. The direct role of solar electromagnetism on earthlights is, however, unknown. Some researchers are still trying to understand the relationship between solar activity and UFO sightings in the context of how it influences the physics of plasma.[20]

The notion that UFOs could be linked to geophysical activity became more firmly established during the 1980s. Paul Devereux published an important book[21] describing his research in 1982, based on extensive fieldwork done in the United Kingdom. He was able to establish, through in-depth cases studies, the full connection between earthlights, and the phenomenology of UFO sightings. Devereux showed that abnormal geophysical activities had occurred during a UFO wave in the United Kingdom, a time when earthlights were positively observed. The earthlights behavior was in turn found consistent with witnesses' description of UFOs. Devereux also noted some strange connections, a kind of two-way street, between the witnesses' state of mind and the behavior of earthlights. Specifically, the intense electromagnetic forces from earthlights seemed to affect the perception of witnesses, and somehow the witnesses seemed able to influence the behavior of the earthlights themselves.

In parallel, the Canadian researcher Michael Persinger was studying the impact of electromagnetic energy on the human the brain. He found that electromagnetism can induce people into altered states of consciousness, and that visionary experiences can be the outcome of such events. Not only can earthlights be perceived as UFOs in the sky, but they could also indicate that UFO witnesses are prone to seeing things that might not be what they appear to be. In other words, although earthlights are real physical objects, they can also induce hallucinations and therefore cause the witnesses to unknowingly report events that are both real and imagined. From the mid-1970s to the end of the 1980s, Persinger published a number of research findings in scientific journals[22] and a book[23] linking the psychological and neurological dimensions of UFOs sightings with unusual geomagnetic activities. His research was later summarized in two comprehensive publications.[24] Persinger's research has had a significant impact in reinforcing the notion that the UFO experience is closely related to electromagnetism.

During the 1990s and early 2000s, other researchers were able to further reinforce the link between electromagnetism and UFO sightings. Using in-depth qualitative case studies, Albert Budden[25] and Keith Partain[26] separately found a very strong correlation between UFO experiences and electromagnetism, including the sighting of what appeared to be non-human entities. Both Budden and Partain, like Persinger, found that an electromagnetically induced altered state of consciousness was very much present in many UFO and "alien" sightings. Budden was also able to show that artificial sources of electromagnetism, such as power distribution stations, telecommunication towers, radars, etc, are playing a role in inducing altered states of consciousness.

Finally, in 2000, the British Ministry of Defence ordered a review of about 10,000 UFO reports under the title *Unidentified*

Aerial Phenomena in the UK Air Defence Region. [27] The report, also known as the Condign Report, was declassified in 2005 and publically released in 2006. The report came to the conclusion that "[t]he relevance of plasma and magnetic fields to UAP [Unidentified Aerial Phenomena] were an unexpected feature of the study."[28] The report states quite clearly that:

> Considerable evidence exists to support the thesis that the events are almost certainly attributable to physical, electrical and magnetic phenomena in the atmosphere, mesosphere and ionosphere. They appear to originate due to more than one set of weather and electrically charged conditions and are observed so infrequently as to make them unique to the majority of observers. There seems to be a strong possibility that at least some of the events may be triggered by meteor re-entry, the meteors neither burning up completely nor impacting as meteorites, but forming buoyant plasmas. The conditions and method of formation of electrically-charged plasmas and the scientific rational for sustaining them for significant periods is incomplete or not fully understood.[29]

Furthermore, the report underlines that "close proximity of plasma fields can adversely affect a vehicle or person […] These result in the observer sustaining (and later describing and retaining) his or her own vivid, but mainly incorrect, description of what is experienced. Some observers are likely to be more susceptible to these fields than others, and may suffer extend memory retention and repeat experiences. This is suggested to be a key factor in influencing the more extreme reports found in the media and are clearly believed by the 'victims.'"[30] The report also states that Soviet Union scientists had already established a link between UFOs and plasma-related phenomenon.[31]

There is no doubt that the electromagnetic dimension of the UFO experience goes beyond mere speculation. There is a significant empirical base, using both quantitative and qualitative data, to confirm the important role that electromagnetism plays. There seems to be little doubt that a number of previously unexplainable UFO sightings can be explained as "earthlights," atmospheric plasma, and electromagnetically induced altered states of consciousness. It is also important to realize that these findings are not only embedded in known physics and the empirical data of the UFO experience, but they are also providing a consistent explanation for the fundamental elusiveness of the phenomenon. Earthlights and atmospheric plasma are transient material effects, but they are not truly solid objects. Similarly, sincere, honest, and credible witnesses could report experiences for which there seemed to be no physical evidence. The apparent discrepancy between the quality of the witness accounts and the lack of physical evidence could thus be accounted for.

The key idea to keep in mind here is that electromagnetism seems somehow to play an important role in the UFO phenomenon. This does not mean that it plays a role in every sighting, nor that it is a necessary condition for a UFO event to occur. It is probably safer to say that electromagnetism is an important *enabler* in the UFO experience. In any event, this is where the majority of evidence points, but more research is still needed to develop a clearer understanding of the physical aspects of the UFO phenomenon.

What the Government Knows
Some people argue that "the government" actually knows much more about UFOs than they are willing to tell us. This usually refers to military and intelligence agencies of the United States government. But the governments of other countries have also investigated, or are still investigating, UFO reports. What do they know about UFOs? Do they come to a different conclusion than the one emerging from the United States government?

In fact, other governments of the world who seriously studied UFOs, at one point or another, came to very similar conclusions to that of United States government. The final report of the well-known U.S. Air Force Project Blue Book states that "(1) no UFO reported, investigated, and evaluated by the Air Force has ever given any indication of threat to our national security; (2) there has been no evidence submitted to or discovered by the Air Force that sightings categorized as 'unidentified' represent technological developments or principles beyond the range of present-day scientific knowledge; and (3) there has been no evidence indicating that sightings categorized as 'unidentified' are extraterrestrial vehicles."[32]

The same pattern of conclusions is apparent in the other English-speaking countries, which are close not only in terms of language, but in terms of bureaucratic culture and military cooperation. There is a significant interest about UFOs in the 1950s, which gradually declines over time. They all came, sooner or later, to the conclusion that UFOs represented no danger, even if some of those reports were quite odd and bizarre. The study of such phenomenon is deemed outside the purview of the military, and may have only limited scientific interest. Hence, far from being perceived as something important, it has been the rule that the military is happy to "pass the buck" on UFO "stuff" to someone else. Canada was the first one to do so in 1967,[33] then the United States in 1969-1970, Australia[34] in 1996, the United Kingdom[35] in 2009, and New Zealand[36] in 2011. In terms of making files available to those interested in the study of UFOs, the United States kicked off the trend by making the Blue Book material available in the early to mid-1970s. If there is any blame to assign, it would be towards those other countries that took so long to make those reports publically available to UFO researchers. Canada only did so in 2005, while Britain made the move in 2008, Australia and New Zealand joining in 2011.

The pattern noted with English-speaking countries is also found in Europe, although there is a bit more variation because there are more countries involved, and they represent a wider set of bureaucratic cultures. From the "I do not care" approach of Ireland,[37] which ceased to collect UFO reports in the 1980s, to the publically funded civilian research done in cooperation with UFO research organizations, which has been the approach in

France[38] and Sweden, [39] and everything in between, they all have the same message: UFOs do not constitute a threat to national security, and this subject is not something that should be studied by the military; it is something for scientists and interested citizens. Various countries came to such a conclusion at various times, starting with France in the 1950s to Belgium[40] in the early 1990s, usually in the aftermath of a wave of UFO sightings. Once more, there is no big "hush-hush" about UFOs, only official indifference with various degrees of "passing the buck" to interested citizens.

In general, governments in Latin America have a relatively open policy about UFOs, dating back to the late 1970s in the case of Uruguay[41] to the more recent actions taken by the Brazilian[42] and Argentinian[43] governments. In the end, the same pattern noted elsewhere is present in Latin America, namely that it is construed as a scientific problem for those interested in studying it, but it is not a military issue even if the military may be the point of contact to collect reports on UFOs and do preliminary analysis.

Some other governments faced unexplainable UFO events, and officially investigated them, but without engaging in long-term research efforts. They also stated in one way or another that they could not explain such events, but they were not too concerned in terms of national security. For instance, in 1989 the Guatemalan government had to deal with a UFO wave and responded that "we don't fully discount the sightings, in fact, we're a little concerned. But there is no proof of anything."[44] In Iran in 1976, after the Imperial Air Force chased a UFO, it was concluded that "there was no apparent explanation for what the pilot did see," but that newspapers also exaggerated what happened.[45] In Portugal, dealing with an unexplainable UFO sighting in 1982, the government concluded after their investigation that "the scientific team studied all the data and the three pilot reports, and after a meeting of all thirty investigators in Porto, in 1984, the group provided a written analysis of more than 170 pages. They did everything they could to understand this case, but they could not find an explanation for it. They concluded that the object remained unidentified."[46]

Once one combines other countries' conclusions about UFOs into a wider holistic assessment, then a similar view to the United States government's perspective emerges:

1. unexplainable UFOs do not constitute a threat to national security;
2. they do not seem to be technological devices;
3. there are indeed very weird cases that might be of interest to some, but they are also very difficult to study scientifically because of their elusive character and the paucity of physical evidence; and,
4. it is not the mandate of a military organization to conduct long-term and difficult scientific study on non-security related matters.

So, where does this leave us? The ETH remains without physical evidence to support itself, and the physical evidence about UFOs points in a different direction, however incomplete it may be. The governments around the world do not know any more than we do. And yet, there are still many fascinating cases that are hard to explain. A small number of UFO researchers have actually advocated since the late 1960s that the UFO phenomenon could be paranormal events, and thus provide a possible explanation about their weird nature. But where does this approach stand today?

Chapter 2
Paranormal Research and UFOs

UFO stories often involve very strange events that are hard to explain—and hard to distinguish from more "classic" paranormal experiences. For instance, in January 1974,[47] a man in Bedfordshire, United Kingdom, was making tea in his home around 11 PM. He suddenly felt the need to look outside. As he came out, he saw in the night sky a red light moving up and down rapidly and erratically. He quickly called his mother and his brother to come out of the house to have a look. All three observed the red light wobbling around for about ten minutes. Then it dropped from the sky like a stone and disappeared. His experience included both a premonition or telepathic experience and a strange event in the night sky. The two events were inseparable as without the sudden urge to look outside there would have been no UFO observation that night.

Then consider this other UFO experience. In the spring of 1966,[48] a young couple renting a small house in a semi-forested area of Woodstock in New York State noticed six greenish lights about 6 feet in diameter in a nearby field. On another occasion they saw something flying close to their car and move towards a wooded area while making a high-pitch sound like the drone of a vacuum cleaner. They heard these sounds many times over a period of several months. Then one afternoon the sound seemed to stop moving and stayed stationary over the house. The woman examined all the electrical equipment in the house but could not find the source of the sound. It seemed to be located in a wall of the house. The couple verified that from outside of the house they could not see anything strange on the wall. But when they looked around at a nearby field, they saw a green light and a smaller red one moving away from each other until they both disappeared. Already frightened by the experience, they then heard a man's voice and the sounds of someone walking. They panicked at that point, but the noise and sound eventually stopped. The next day, they noticed that the grass near their house was flat and scorched, and it did not recover much during the entire summer. Was this a UFO encounter or was it a poltergeist? Does it even make sense to try making such a distinction between a UFO and poltergeist event?

These are just two examples—and not particularly extraordinary ones—of how the UFO experience seems to be intertwined with paranormal events. Other UFO observations are more spectacular, at times involving many people with multiple strange events over a longer period of time. One of the best-known, large-scale paranormal UFO events is the one investigated by the late John Keel in 1966 and 1967 and presented in his book *The Mothman Prophecies*, published in 1975. In this book, Keel relates the story of his investigation of a UFO wave experienced by a small West Virginia town, Point Pleasant, and the paranormal events surrounding it. There were poltergeist disturbances, people having premonitions of all kinds, apparitions of strange beings, including the Mothman, etc. All these events occurred before the main bridge in the town, which crossed the Ohio River, suddenly collapsed killing many people on the spot. The UFO wave and the string of paranormal events ceased shortly thereafter. Although Keel offers a nuanced explanation in his book about the origin of the UFO wave at Pleasant Point, he clearly felt that the UFOs and the other paranormal events represented some sort of premonition of the bridge tragedy.

The study of UFO experiences as a paranormal event
The first serious author to suggest that UFOs might be some kind of paranormal effect was the famous psychoanalyst Carl Jung (1875-1961) in his book *Flying Saucers: A modern myth of things seen in the skies*, originally published in German in 1958 and translated in English in 1959. Jung looked into the UFO phenomenon through the lenses of social psychology and eventually concluded that UFOs are probably shared mental images triggered by socially shared anxieties. For Jung, our anxieties with modern life and the dangers of a nuclear confrontation during the Cold War led many people to see flying saucers in the sky, a round shape that reminds us of our desire to have our life back the way it was;

to complete the circle so to speak, by symbolically representing unity and stability.

Jung's analysis is complex and subtle. He acknowledged that UFOs have a degree of physical reality, too. This led him to briefly suggest that psychokinesis (PK) or mind-over-matter could be a potential explanation for UFOs, but he ultimately rejected that idea because it was contrary to our understanding of modern physics.[49] However, he also noted that the "psychic situation of mankind and the UFO phenomenon as a physical reality bear no recognizable causal relationship to one another, but they seem to coincide in a meaningful manner."[50] For those who are familiar with Jung's psychology, meaningful coincidences are important events that illustrate a phenomenon that he called "synchronicity." For him, synchronicity is the observable effect of psychic powers in action at a given time, such as thinking about something and that something happening shortly thereafter without apparent related cause. This is an important idea in the sense that the paranormal dimension of UFOs could be not only a matter of strange phenomena but also a matter of *strange timing*.

More than a decade later, the paranormal approach to UFOs got a serious boost with the publication in 1969 of *Passport to Magonia: From folklore to flying saucers* by Jacques Vallée. At the time Vallée had already established himself as a serious scientist who thought that UFOs might be spaceships from another world. He studied a series of historical cases describing encounters with enchanted beings such as elves, fairies, and leprechauns, and compared them with modern cases of close encounters of the third kind (i.e. meeting the occupants of UFOs). He found that there were many similarities between them, including strange physical sensations, a dream-like atmosphere, loss of a sense of time, meaningless behavior of the entities, nonsense discussions with the entities, telepathic communications, levitation, etc. In light of these numerous strange similarities with the UFO experience, he came to believe that the UFO experience might indeed be a paranormal or parapsychological phenomenon.

As mentioned earlier, John Keel's investigation of the events in Point Pleasant led him to think that the UFO phenomenon was difficult to distinguish from the paranormal. But even before that, Keel had written a lesser-known book in 1970 entitled *Operation Trojan Horse* in which he suggested that something paranormal or parapsychological was an integral part of the UFO experience. Keel separately collected reports and observations that were quite similar to the descriptions that Vallée offered in *Passport to Magonia*. Keel came to conclude that if there were actual entities involved, they seemed to be more of a psychical nature, calling them "ultraterrestrials" or trans-dimensional beings. Because it discounted the ETH, *Operation Trojan Horse*, however, was not well received at the time.

By the 1970s, other authors and researchers also noted that there was something paranormal about the UFO experience. One of the pioneers of modern UFOlogy, astronomer J. Allen Hynek, who had been the U.S. Air Force's official UFO researcher since the 1950s, also admitted that UFOs could not be understood without incorporating their paranormal or parapsychological dimension.[51] In a newly re-discovered letter that Hynek wrote to psychical researchers in Toronto in 1977, he stated: "I am being driven, somewhat reluctantly to the feeling that many UFOs are caused by our own psychic energy somehow interacting with matter."[52] Around the same time, Jerome Clark and Loren Coleman[53] also noted that UFO reports often had a paranormal dimension. Somewhat inspired by Jung's ideas, the two authors went a bit further, proposing that the UFO phenomenon could be a materialized expression of unconscious tensions; they wrote: "the 'objective' manifestations [of UFOs] are psychokinetically generated byproducts of those unconscious processes which shape a culture's vision of the otherworld. Existing only temporarily, they are at best only quasiphysical."[54] In other words, they concluded that UFOs seem to be the result of psychokinesis. This idea is inspired from scientific parapsychology. Paranormal events, which are known by the term "psi" in parapsychology, are considered to be the manifestations of deep unconscious mental dynamics. Clark and Coleman suggested that maybe such dynamics exist at the collective level, too. Later, however, Clark came to see the extra-terrestrial hypothesis as a more satisfying explanation for

UFO reports. It is interesting to note that an American defense scientist also published in 1979 an interesting paper where the possibility of UFOs as collective psi events could be explained in terms quantum physics. His paper was even presented at a MUFON conference.[55]

Scott Rogo, one of the very few parapsychologists who seriously studied the UFO phenomenon, also found a number of parallels between the UFO experience and the poltergeist disturbances. He published his findings in 1977 in *The Haunted Universe*. Rogo noted that one common pattern within the UFO experience is that our thoughts are sent back to us.[56] For instance, people would talk about UFOs, and then they would see one later on. People who see UFOs also often tend to have multiple experiences over the years. Furthermore, people tend to see what they are culturally conditioned to expect. For instance, people saw "airships" in the skies of North America at the end of the 19th century, a few years before they were flown; Scandinavians saw many ghost rockets in the sky just after the end of World War II and before much more powerful rockets were available to reach Scandinavia; a few years before the launch of the space age with the Soviet Sputnik satellite many people saw things in the sky that were interpreted as spaceships. In poltergeist disturbances, it is very common to have events expressing our thoughts. For example, someone who wants to leave the house after having enough of the disturbance may end up finding his shoes in the freezer. Poltergeist events are not experienced in the same way everywhere because cultural interpretations vary. Hence, the social dynamics by which the phenomenon is "displaced" will also vary. For instance, in Brazil poltergeist events are oftentimes construed as an outcome of local spiritualized practices, where the contacted soul of the departed is responding in an angered way, while in Europe it is perceived at first as a strange and unexplainable event.

Also in 1977, Pierre Viéroudy's *Ces ovnis qui annoncent le surhomme* (*UFOs Announcing the Arrival of the Superhuman*) was published in France. This book proposes one of the best syntheses of research on UFOs and parapsychology done at the time, linking Jung's ideas, anthropological and sociological observations, models and theories from scientific parapsychology, and UFOlogical material. But more important, he conducted field research where he and a few colleagues mentally "provoked" the creation of UFOs in the night sky of France and took some pictures of them. His field research, however, was never successfully repeated.

Another French researcher, the sociologist Bertrand Méheust, conducted an extensive study of pre-World War II science-fiction comics and found many similarities with the stories later told by UFO experiencers. His findings were published in 1978 in his book *Science-fiction et soucoupes volantes* (*Science Fiction and Flying Saucers*). It should be understood that Méheust did not find a link between those who had reported UFO experiences and the reading of science-fiction comic books. In a number of cases, the UFO report came from the United States while the comic describing a very similar scene appeared in a relatively obscure and discontinued French science-fiction magazine that had appeared decades earlier. For Méheust, having descriptions of UFO events and comic book representations so separated in space and time suggested something akin to socially shared telepathy.

In the 1980s, other researchers added new pieces to help us understand the paranormal dimension of the UFO puzzle. In 1983, Jenny Randles[57] noted a significant strangeness in many UFO experiences; this varied from the witness's feeling the urge to look in the sky to meeting and interacting with odd entities. In many of these situations, the experiencers were in an altered state of consciousness, from being slightly absent-minded to being in a deep trance. This is what she came to call the "Oz factor." In 1988 Berthold Schwartz, a psychiatrist, published *UFO Dynamics: Psychiatric and Psychic Aspects of the UFO Syndrome*, where he presented a well-researched analysis of UFO experiences viewed as parapsychological events. For him, parapsychology was a much better fit to explain what happened to his patients than the extra-terrestrial hypothesis.

Also in 1988, Manfred Cassirer published a small book entitled

Parapsychology and the UFO.[58] He made an exhaustive inventory of similarities between events studied by parapsychologists and those studied by ufologists. Among the similarities he identified are that the photographs of such events tended to be fuzzy, as if what is photographed is not fully material. There was also equipment malfunction when in the presence of both phenomena, as well as extra-sensory perceptions (ESP), strange noises, and objects that moved in defiance of the laws of physics. Others over the years have also pursued the notion that the UFO experience could be a form of psi or parapsychological event,[59] confirming and adding to findings from previous researchers.[60]

The strange connection between electromagnetism and the paranormal

As noted in the previous chapter, electromagnetism can affect the human mind. But, for quite some time research has also pointed towards the possibility that the human mind can somehow influence electrical and magnetic systems too. This would be a two-way street. Parapsychology has been studying such effects by testing how human intentions can influence electromagnetic systems. The university-based Princeton Engineering Anomalies Research (PEAR) lab, which is now continuing its research as the International Consciousness Research Laboratories (ICRL),[61] has been a pioneer in this type of research. In one instance, they conducted a series of experiments with a wheeled robot that changed direction randomly every second and asked people try to influence telepathically the on-board random number generator so that the robot would move in a specified direction. This and other experiments they conducted have shown that the human mind can indeed affect sensitive binary electromagnetic systems.[62]

Beyond the work done by PEAR, there is a significant literature on the topic, which is itself based on empirical research from a variety of fields. Some of the most fascinating research about the interaction between the human mind and electromagnetic systems is the research on poltergeist events, known in the field as Recurrent Spontaneous Psychokinetic (RSPK) effects, and hauntings.[63] Examples include a light bulb burning out when someone is in a negative state of mind, electrical equipment starting up or shutting down without apparent cause, etc.

Researcher Paul Devereux has described having experiences with earthlights that seemed to interact with him. When he thought of the earthlight moving in a specific direction, for example, it actually did so. This was an important finding, suggesting that the human mind can indeed affect things "out there" in the physical world. Neuroscientist Michael Persinger also researched the similarities between events that occurred during poltergeist cases and UFO experiences.[64] He found that when the human brain is exposed to high levels of electromagnetism, the normal processes of the human mind are disturbed and can result in hallucinations, an altered state of consciousness, falling unconscious, and visionary experiences, It can also potentially enhance parapsychological abilities. In her own work, Dr. Pamela Heath[65] found in her exhaustive analysis of mind-over-matter that the physiological and psychological effects described by Persinger are often associated with increased PK performances.

Unfortunately, most previous studies have not operationalized these ideas much beyond looking at the observable similarities between UFO events and paranormal ones. If indeed UFO phenomena are paranormal events, then one should be able to use the conceptual tools, models, and theories of parapsychology and apply them to UFO cases. By doing so, it becomes possible to move away from simply describing mysterious UFO events, and start moving towards explaining them. The question, therefore, becomes how can we start explaining more rigorously the UFO phenomenon from a parapsychological perspective?

Chapter 3
The Parapsychological Hypothesis

On October 28, 1968, a medical doctor in Southern France, known only as Dr. X to protect his identity, injured his leg while cutting wood. Three days later, on November 2, he was woken up around 4 AM by a storm and saw his child pointing towards the window. When the doctor looked through the window, he saw two disk-shaped objects glowing and emitting lightning strikes. The two objects eventually merged to become a single object, whereupon a powerful light appeared and illuminated the doctor's face. Suddenly there was a loud bang and the object disappeared into thin air. When he woke up his wife, she noted that his leg wound had disappeared. After a few days, he noted that his older wounds from the war in Algeria were also gone.

A few days later, he noticed a triangular-shaped red spot around his navel. His child also displayed the same skin pigmentation. It eventually went away. The event had a strong psychological impact on the entire family: "They seem to have acquired an almost mystical acceptance of the events of life and death, which is puzzling to those who had known them previously."[66] Furthermore, after that incident, they also reported having telepathic experiences, the levitation of an object, and the malfunctioning of electrical and electronic equipment.

The experience of Dr. X is both personal and impersonal. The healing of his wound and the poltergeist-like events in his house afterward could be seen as psychokinesis centered on him. The UFO part of his experience seems impersonal and disconnected from anything around him. This is an example of a well-known and well-researched UFO event[67] that seems worthy of an investigation by parapsychologists. Yet most parapsychologists have kept a safe distance from the UFO subject, afraid of being associated with "alien and spaceship enthusiasts." Or, as John Keel once noted, "[a] parapsychologist will travel halfway around the world to investigate a poltergeist case, but if his next-door neighbor is bathed in a beam of light on a lonely back road, the scientist will regard it as nothing more than a dinner table anecdote."[68]

A too common misunderstanding
This book is based on what I called the "parapsychological hypothesis," which I wish to distinguish from the paranormal hypothesis regarding the origins of the UFO phenomenon. Thus far I have used both terms more or less interchangeably, but it is now appropriate to give them a narrower meaning. Modern parapsychology was created in the 1930s under the leadership of professor Joseph Banks Rhine. From the beginning, it was determined that parapsychology, as a discipline, would distance itself from previous research on the paranormal. The main reason was that parapsychologists did not want to include in their research any notion that non-human entities (souls of the departed, ghosts, fairies, spirits, demons, etc.) would be behind various paranormal phenomena. They preferred to see paranormal events as just the effects of natural human potentials, which are poorly understood but not supernatural. At least, that is the official position of scientific parapsychology.

There are several reasons for this decision. First, if one wants to study something scientifically, then it requires that the object of study can be measured and observed so that patterns can be found. Human behavior can be assessed from a relatively objective standpoint; spirits or aliens that would call the shots as to how and when they show up cannot be scientifically studied, as there is no possibility to establish a "natural" pattern about their behavior. Furthermore, to advance knowledge one needs to start from the known and move towards the unknown. We know a fair bit about human thinking, emotions, and behavior; we have absolutely no objective knowledge about what any spirit or alien might think, feel, or do. Lastly, there is no need to hypothesize the existence of human beings because we know they exist; while on the other hand the existence of any spirit or aliens remains conjectural and relies solely on speculation.

For the very same reasons, the parapsychological hypothesis on UFOs does not incorporate any notions that UFOs are related to "dimensional beings," "ultraterrestrials," or any other non-human entities. The point here is not that speculation about non-human entities is correct or incorrect, but rather that such speculation has not led to any new understanding about the UFO phenomenon. Hence, the basic assumption of the parapsychological hypothesis I will explore here is that humans are responsible for subconsciously producing paranormal phenomena—including UFOs. In this light, there are no valid and logical reasons for scientific parapsychologists to ignore the UFO enigma.

The parapsychological notion of "psi"
Parapsychologists have studied the paranormal rigorously and have devised the concept of "psi" to describe the paranormal. Scientific parapsychologists usually consider that there are two forms of psi. One involves the acquisition of information through non-normal means, usually referred to as Extra-Sensory Perception (ESP), and covers a series of phenomena such as telepathy, premonition, and precognition, as well as remote viewing or clairvoyance, etc. The second form of psi is called Psycho-Kinesis (PK), and refers to "mind-over-matter" events such as calling the right number in throwing dice, causing strange electronic malfunctions, moving objects without physical force, producing poltergeist disturbances, healing people, and materializing objects out of thin air.

In the last 80 years parapsychologists have discovered some patterns about how psi works (either ESP or PK). For instance, strong emotions tend to play a role. Telepathy seems more common among people who have affection for one another, and poltergeist disturbances often seem to be linked to strong unspoken family tensions. Parapsychologists have also noted that premonitions are more likely to occur the more dangerous or important the situation. In the same vein, they have shown that if an experimenter believes in psi, the results tend to be positive, while a skeptical experimenter will tend to get negative results; parapsychologists label this the sheep-goat effect.

So the subconscious or unconscious seems to play a key role in producing psi effects. People who are more intuitive like artists,

35

namely people more in touch with their unconscious thoughts and feelings, tend to score higher on ESP tests. Likewise, psi effects tend to be more frequent when people are in an altered state of consciousness, i.e. when their unconscious is allowed to come to the fore (temporarily absent minded, half asleep, hypnotized, in trance, etc.).

Parapsychologists have also noted that psi effects produced in laboratory tend to be very small, while psi effects occurring in people's normal life tend to be much more visible. They call this last form of psi effect "spontaneous." In laboratory experiments, it is the conscious mind that tries to "force" the unconscious to "deliver," even if it is not ready to do so. But in daily life, the unconscious "calls the shots" when it is ready, and "delivers" it spontaneously.

Parapsychologists have also joined forces with some quantum physicists, and have developed a number of interesting ideas. One of them, borrowed from modern physics, is that matter is more than mass and energy; it is also information, such as speed, direction, relative position, internal organization, etc. Seen from this angle, the distinction between the ESP and PK forms of psi may not be necessary, as psi would then be simply about accessing or modifying information about either ideas or objects through non-normal means.

How could these findings about psi be helpful to study the UFO phenomenon? As noted in the previous chapter, the UFO experience has shown over the years that there are often obvious paranormal aspects to it. Many of them are fully in line with what parapsychology is studying, e.g. involving telepathy, psychokinetic levitation, poltergeist-like disturbances, psychokinetic self-healing, the impact of altered states of consciousness on psi, visionary experiences, clairvoyance, premonitions, etc. Most of what happened to Dr. X lies squarely within the realm of parapsychology. These personal paranormal experiences linked to UFO cases can be studied as psi effects.

But there is also an impersonal aspect to the UFO experience, actually seeing an object "out there" in the sky. Could it also be explained as psi?

The notion of social psi[69]

Something called "social psi" has been proposed by the well-known and respected parapsychologist Dean Radin.[70] This notion implies that when many people are engaged in a common experience, they collectively contribute to, and are affected by, psi effects. Such social psi effects seem to have a dynamic of their own, irreducible to individual psi dynamics. Already in the 1950s, the parapsychologist Nandor Fodor described social forms of psi effects in his field research. He wrote of...

> ...death coaches driven by ghost drivers, and many other human, semi-human, and animal apparitions that in old English families are the heralds of impending death. They add "body" to the Family Gestalt. The older the family, the stronger the Gestalt. Nebulous and ill-defined as it necessarily must be, the concept of the Family Gestalt unites a variety of ill-assorted phenomena of folklore with psychical research.[71]

In the 1960s and 1970s, some parapsychologists engaged in group séances to invoke spirits and ghosts who were the product of the imagination of the group of people in the room, not the involvement of a disincarnate entity. The most famous of such experiments was conducted in Toronto, Canada, over several months by Iris Owen and Margaret Sparrow in the early 1970s. Over time, they produced what they considered an "artificial ghost," which the group had deliberately imaged, but who seemed to communicate with them through raps and knocking (PK effect). A number of other PK effects were noted, such as the table they were using lifting by itself; some of the participants even had unexplainable things moving in their own house after the séance, etc. The British parapsychologist Kenneth Batcheldor conducted comparable collective experiments and was able to have his group affect electrical equipment, and in particular a lamp's lighting. So strength in numbers seems to apply to psi, too.

Psi effects noted during all these empirical observations could be qualified as "impersonal" in that they are interpreted as being made of an amalgamation of intentions and unconscious processes by several individuals. As the parapsychologist Scott Rogo noted:

> There is another psychological factor which comes into play during group PK practices which I felt Batcheldor fails to appreciate... group-PK effects are often directed by a collective mind created by the sitters. By joining forces, several people may actually form some sort of semiautonomous will or mind that directs the PK. Now this "entity" is not "owned" by or dependent upon any single group member. It is, on the contrary, semi independent of all of them. A PK group, therefore, can overcome ownership inhibition because the PK is really being architectured by an ego-alien personality.[72]

One important aspect of social psi is that it offers the possibility to have many people involved in spontaneous parapsychological events without any particular individual being responsible for it. In other words, while social psi effects are produced by a group of people, they are experienced by the individuals as an impersonal set of events. Many people, when they report a UFO, often experience a mixture of personal relationships with the events (such as personal visionary experience and telepathy) and an impersonal reality at the same time (like seeing something that has the appearance of a manufactured object). The parapsychological notion of social psi could account for such situations without having to involve any non-human entities.

If we go back to the experience of Dr. X, let's take note that the year 1968 was one of high social and emotional intensity in France. In May of that year, major university student protests erupted in Paris; the students seized a number of important buildings in the city. Strikers from major labor unions soon joined them. The situation eventually deteriorated into major street fights with the police over several days. Many were afraid that France was facing yet another revolution. The government eventually fell and agreed to meet the demands of the students to reform the higher education system. These events of May 1968 led to the worst civil unrest in France in decades. Interestingly, the law to reform higher education and attempt to heal a serious social wound in French society came into effect on November 12, 1968, just a few days after the healing events experienced by Dr. X. There is here an interesting combination of personal and impersonal symbolic synchronicity. Could it also be an example of social psi effect? Could Dr. X's own psi capability have gotten entangled with the social psi forces, leading to a strange mixture of personal and impersonal UFO events in November 1968?

There is no easy answer to this question. It was in the end a relatively circumscribed event, and although first class researchers extensively investigated it, the focus remained on Dr. X and his family. It was not researched with a broader view; that's the case for almost all UFO investigations. It is no surprise then that the impersonal dimension of the UFO phenomenon remains the least understood part of this enigma.

As already noted, it is quite difficult to understand UFO events simply because very often there is not enough information available. But there is a good bit of public information involving UFO waves or flaps, which involve many cases in the same area at the same time. This makes flaps and waves an ideal starting point in our investigation into the parapsychological underpinnings of the UFO experience. So the next question is: how can we study a large-scale UFO event from a parapsychological perspective?

Recurrent Spontaneous Psychokinesis as a template to study UFO waves[73]

The experience of Dr. X was not only spontaneous, but both personal and impersonal. Parapsychologists have studied intensely only a few forms of spontaneous psi events. Among them are poltergeist disturbances, which are called Recurrent Spontaneous Psychokinesis (RSPK) in parapsychology. Here again, parapsychologists do not consider RSPK the result of some non-human entity's activities, but rather the result of out-of-control unconscious emotions that for some reason are expressed through psychokinesis and other forms of psi effect.

One of the most interesting and recent models to study RSPK was developed by the physicist Walter von Lucadou. It is particularly useful because it integrates not just the people experiencing the disturbances, but various social dynamics, the impersonal dimension. In other words, his model offers the possibility of combining in a coherent framework the effects of both personal psi and social psi. This model offers a rare opportunity to investigate the UFO phenomenon from a parapsychological standpoint, as it can accommodate both the personal and impersonal aspects. But first, what are RSPK events or poltergeists?

Poltergeist activities are among the most complex and elusive of paranormal events, and share many similarities with the UFO experience. They happen spontaneously and without warning, and are often characterized by inexplicable banging in the walls, levitating objects, the independent behavior of electrical equipment, unexplainable voices, teleportation of objects, and in a few cases people hearing footsteps or reporting marks left on the ground, etc. Witnesses often provide conflicting accounts, and it is not uncommon for faking and hoaxing to be mixed in with the "real" events, a situation that is very difficult to explain. Parapsychology has been trying to make sense of these events for more than a century.

Consider, for example, one of the most famous 20th century poltergeist cases, the Enfield Poltergeist.[74] The story began in a social housing unit in Enfield, a northern suburb of London, in August 1977, when a recently divorced mother of four was told by her children that their bed was shaking unexplainably. Little worried, she did nothing about it. The next night, she heard unexplainable noises and saw a chest drawer sliding along the floor by itself. That's when she realized that something strange was going on.[75] Thinking that there might be a burglar in the house, she ran to a neighbor's house with her children and called the police. When the police arrived, they found no burglar, but one police officer saw a chair moving by itself. The next day, more objects were seen moving by themselves. Another neighbor decided to call the newspaper, and in the days that followed a number of reporters and police officers claimed to have witnessed very strange events at the house.[76]

A journalist decided to call the Society for Psychical Research (SPR) to see if they would investigate. The case was assigned to Maurice Grosse who noted that the disturbances were focused on one of the children, Janet, who was 11 at the time. Among other things, she was seen levitating above her bed. For Grosse, there was no doubt that it was a legitimate poltergeist case. The investigators suggested to the mother that she try communicating with the poltergeist by rapping and knocking; the story is that it was apparently responsive to such communications.[77]

Later on the American illusionist Milbourne Christopher also investigated the case, but from a much more skeptical point of view. He did not witness anything unusual and became very suspicious that Janet might be involved in trickery.[78] Interestingly, Guy Lyon Playfair, in his book on the case, noted when referring to Christopher's investigation that "it almost seemed that the poltergeist was out to incriminate her, by producing third-rate phenomena in the presence of a first-rate observer."[79] The events stopped in 1979. Janet eventually admitted in a 1980 TV interview that there was some trickery involved on her part, but maintained that most of it was genuine.[80] Later, a more critical analysis of the events suggested that a lot more trickery might have been involved.[81] By 1992, the BBC produced *Ghostwatch*, a mockumentary largely inspired by the Enfield Poltergeist.

The Model of Pragmatic Information

The Model of Pragmatic Information (MPI), proposed by psychologist and physicist Walter von Lucadou, presents new opportunities for parapsychology to explore RSPK events from a fresh perspective. He noted that RSPK events go through four generic phases: they first tend to increase in intensity, then peak, followed by a decline, until finally they disappear. But he noticed that the variations in the intensity of psi events are fundamentally related to the types of people who become involved in the events. In other words, the dynamics of RSPK events are entirely intertwined with social dynamics; it is both a matter of personal and impersonal events.

The Enfield Poltergeist story follows relatively well what the MPI predicts in terms of how a RSPK event tends to unfold in four phases:

(1) **Surprise.** Typically, the event involves an individual who is experiencing significant emotional turmoil (oftentimes a teenager or a pre-teen, but not always), but because of some social dynamics cannot express it. The person's PK (banging on walls, moving objects, etc.) becomes an alternate way to communicate about his or her psychological turmoil (the pragmatic information). That person is called the "focus person" because the psi events are focused, or localized, around him or her. But the people surrounding the focus person also play a role in the event by their surprise and by their belief that the event is caused by some sort of malevolent non-human entity (demon, evil spirit, ghost, etc.). In doing so, these people, called the "environment," maintain indeterminacy in the system by avoiding observing the real system at play, namely the psychological turmoil of the focus person. In the Enfield case, Janet was readily identified as the focus person, a pre-teen who was dealing with the fresh divorce of her parents. The events started as surprise, and the neighbors (the environment) quickly began to suspect something paranormal was happening and called the press.

(2) **Displacement.** After some time, the events become known and other people joined in. The first on the scene are typically those who believe in the existence of non-human entities, such as psychics, self-declared parapsychologists, sensationalist journalists, etc. These newcomers are called the "naive observers" because of their belief that non-human entities are responsible for the phenomenon. The naïve observers firmly direct the search away from the actual source (the focus person

and his/her distress) and cause a displacement of attention. This allows the indeterminacy to be maintained, so that the psi phenomenon can continue. This usually occurs in a different and more intense manner, as the message from the focus person seeks to be understood, while the people's attention in the environment is further distracted. In the Enfield case, the phenomenon intensified as the investigation by a journalist and the SPR unfolded (the naïve observers). The SPR investigators actually reinforced the belief that it was a paranormal force by "teaching" the mother how to communicate with the "entity."

(3) **Decline.** Later still, other people join in, but with a much more critical view of the events. They start to assess more carefully what is going on, asking more thorough questions about who is involved, and sometimes introducing measuring instruments. At times they make a connection between the events (which usually have a symbolic meaning) and the unhappiness of the focus person. These people are called the "critical observers." Given that they pay a much closer look at the systems at hand, they reduce the indeterminacy and by doing so the intensity of the phenomenon drops sharply. In the Enfield case, with the arrival of Christopher and other skeptics on the scene (the critical observers), it seems that trickery became much more prevalent. Even Playfair noted that phenomenon seemed to "adjust" to the critical observers.

(4) **Suppression.** At the end, the authorities (police, social services, municipal works, etc.) and society at large get involved because of the disturbances. They usually declare the phenomenon a hoax through the media, often by accusing the focus person and his/her environment of being responsible for the events. With the authorities focusing intensely on the phenomenon, no indeterminacy is left, and no more psi effects occur. Although in the Enfield case the authorities did not use all their weight to dismiss the phenomenon, Janet's public admission of trickery contributed to the suppression of the case, as did further critical research, and ended with the BBC mockumentary, further

damaging the legacy of the case.

The MPI defines psi phenomena as non-local correlations, as expressed in quantum physics. The notion of non-local correlations refers to a phenomenon observed in microphysics where two particles share the same information about their movement without any apparent explanation for such correlation of information. When applied to macrophysics through the MPI, the non-local correlation is done through the sharing of the pragmatic information (i.e., information having a symbolic meaning, and linked to the distress of the focus person in the case of RSPK) by two or more systems (people, objects, energetic systems, etc.).[82] In addition, information is understood in its broader sense to include, for instance, the speed and trajectory of physical objects. The levitation of Janet and the moving of furniture in the Enfield case could have been a way for her to express her unconscious desire to move away from where she lived, to get back to her previous life when her parents were together.

The MPI also postulates that psi phenomena are inherently elusive because, for non-local correlations to occur, at least one of the correlated systems must be in a state of relative indeterminacy; it has to be "loose" and under limited control and order. Along the same lines, the MPI integrates, in its most generic sense, the quantum physics notion of system preparation (i.e. measurement construct), where the very fact of observing a system introduces order into it, and therefore reduces its indeterminacy. This would explain well-known issues that paranormal investigators commonly face when they attempt to measure any paranormal phenomena by taking pictures, videos, voice recordings, thermometers, etc. The phenomenon usually stops until the equipment is packed away, or the measurements are fuzzy and inconclusive compared to what witnesses reported. In other words, measurements tend to "kill" the phenomenon; the more closely a system is observed, the less likely it can produce psi effects. These general principles can also account for why most psi events seem to be linked to deep unconscious processes, where there is a lot of symbolic flux and possibility when compared to the activity of the conscious mind.[83]

The MPI provides not only a predictive description of how RSPK events are likely to unfold, it is also an explanation for them. As noted above, the explanation is built on integrating the parapsychological notion of psi into social dynamics and quantum physics. This framework provides a rare entry point for those interested in studying impersonal anomalous phenomena such as UFOs from a parapsychological perspective. However, the MPI does not answer the most difficult question: unspoken family tensions are not uncommon, so why in some rare cases does it take a psychokinetic form? The necessary parameters enabling such manifestations also remain for the most part unknown. This also holds true for the UFO phenomenon. But if one can at least show that UFO events and RSPK have common characteristics, then there are more reasons to think that they also share a common origin.

One challenge in using the MPI for studying UFO waves, and other more impersonal types of UFO experiences, is to identify who might be the focus person(s). If the experiencer is not the focus person but is merely of one of the individuals in the environment where the impersonal psi effects (i.e. the UFO) are occurring, then who might be the focus? The focus person is defined as someone going through some sort of turmoil but who cannot express it for some reason except through psi effects. But what if the focus is a whole group of people, who generate an impersonal psi effect, then how could we identify them?

One more piece to the puzzle
Psi events, whether they are individual or social, are by definition happening without an observable and direct cause-and-effect. Telepathy, for instance, is just two or more people thinking or feeling the same thing at the same time. If UFO events are also social psi effects, then no one should expect to see any direct and observable cause-and-effect between social tensions and turmoil and the UFO events. However, there are indirect ways to do so, based on the general principles about psi uncovered over the

years by scientific parapsychology. In light of what is known about RSPKs, then the following set of criteria could help us assess not only if a series of UFO events could possibly be unfolding like a poltergeist event, but localizing a possible source of social psi that could account for the more impersonal dimensions as well:

1. The Observation System is Social

For the observation system to be social means that the UFO event received enough attention from the general public to be noted, usually through the mass media. This criterion is based on a number of findings and theories emerging from parapsychology. Psi phenomena are considered to be the outcome of emotional intentions and meaningful events.[84] The key question is, meaningful for whom? In the case of RSPK, someone is trying to attract attention in order to get help. The visible range of psi phenomena is usually a good indicator for assessing to whom the psi effect is directed at—that is, to whom the pragmatic information is directed. Hence, if it is meant to seek help about an impending social tragedy or problem, the information would be directed towards society at large, or a portion thereof, especially if the UFO events "insist" on being known by many. The events related by John Keel in Mount Pleasant, as discussed in the previous chapter, fit well this criterion.

2. Geographical Proximity

Geographical proximity means that large-scale UFO events are more likely to be observed in geographical areas around where the emotional charge, or social tension, is released.[85] This criterion is based on the same notion that the psi effect is information directed by "someone," and that "someone" is seeking the attention of where "somebody" else can be found. Again, using the example from The Mothman Prophecies, the people of Mount Pleasant were unconsciously feeling that something bad was to happen soon, and would have been trying, again unconsciously, to alert someone to the imminent danger.

3. Chronological Proximity

Chronological proximity means that large-scale UFO events are more likely to occur around the same time as the social event causing the social tension. The UFO events can take place either a few days before or after a particularly meaningful event, but the social event would have to be one that packs a significant emotional charge. Yet such an event may not be known publicly at the time of the UFO sightings, in a manner similar to the inner tension lived by the focus person in a poltergeist disturbance. Oftentimes, chronological proximity can only be discovered after the fact, because the source of emotional tension is only known unconsciously,[86] and that, by definition, is not observable. This may include the feeling of "something will happen" but not knowing exactly what it is. In the case of the events of Mount Pleasant, this would be the upcoming bridge tragedy. No one seemed to have been consciously aware that the bridge was structurally unsound. People had a vague intuition of "something," but not precisely what that something was.

4. Symbolic Relationship

Large-scale UFO events oftentimes carry symbolism that can be related to particular events that would carry important emotional tensions. Such symbolism, however, normally emerges from the unconscious and can be quite subtle in nature, oftentimes only comprehensible through lateral forms of thinking, and usually long after the fact. For instance, in a classic RSPK investigation conducted by Nandor Fodor, the focus person "produced" a short rain of violet flowers. After a lengthy interview, Fodor realized that the focus person had been raped when she was young, but never told anyone. He concluded that her unconscious mind expressed itself through psi effects and through lateral thinking, as "violet" and "violate" are almost identical words though they have distinct meanings. The symbolism of a Mothman, to go back to Keel's investigation, involves "people" and "night" (the bridge collapsed at night). Psi effects are the outcome of unconscious processes, and the language of the unconscious is fundamentally symbolic.[87]

Case in point: The 1954 French UFO wave
In 1954, France and many parts of Western Europe experienced a rash of UFO reports. These were reported in the news, and the authorities were asked many times to investigate what was happening. Aimé Michel wrote about the events in a book that would become famous in UFOlogical circles.[88] Interestingly, the titles of the first four chapters use a musical analogy to describe the unfolding of the UFO wave: the Orchestra Tunes Up, Crescendo, Full Orchestra, Diminuendo. This is very similar to how the MPI describes the unfolding of poltergeist events.[89] The wave became a public event in France. Hence, *the observation system was social.*

Donald A. Johnson[90] reanalyzed the data about the 1954 wave using the UFOCAT catalogue, a commonly used UFO sightings catalog created and maintained by the Chicago-based Center for UFO Studies (CUFOS). He noted that the number of UFO sightings for the year 1954 was 3,015, of which about 58% occurred in Europe. The wave was in fact worldwide, but it had a specific peak in October with nearly a third of all sightings (961) in Europe. Of those 961 European cases, 750 occurred in the skies over France, with one particular peak on October 3, and another one on October 15, with about 80 sightings for each date. Although the wave was not exclusively a French UFO wave, it is fair to say that it was indeed centered on France. Hence, *geographical proximity.*

The most interesting element of the wave was its timing. On October 10, 1954, between the French UFO sightings peaks of October 3 and October 15, the *Front de Libération Nationale* (FLN) was informally created by a small group of anti-colonial insurgents in Algeria. As we now know, the FLN waged an extensive political and armed struggle to free Algeria from French colonial rule. This led to a bitter conflict involving more than 500,000 French soldiers, countless victims in Algeria, and something that deeply shocked French society. Although the French Army won on the ground,[91] the FLN won the political battle based on the immorality of colonialism and, in 1962, Algeria gained its independence. Over one million French citizens of European descent living in Algeria had to seek refuge in France to avoid brutal retaliations from the newly formed Algerian authorities. The creation of the FLN in October 1954 was not known to the French public, and even the FLN terrorist actions of November 1954 did not appear to be anything threatening at the time.[92] But the wide scope of the emotional turmoil to come seemed to have been "sensed" unconsciously, as a form of collective premonition. Hence, *chronological proximity*.

Some would argue that this could be a coincidence, though probably an unlikely one. UFO waves are relatively rare events, and when they have a clear peak period, they rarely last more than a few days. The events that the founding of the FLN set in motion had a very deep political, social, and cultural impact on French society[93] —such events are also very rare. Hence, there is a *symbolic relationship* between these events in the form of a "synchronicity" of events in the sky of France and the upcoming tragedy that had been put in motion in Algeria, which would eventually involve all of French society.

The approach that views paranormal phenomena as symbolic and meaningful events has also been taken by Jeffrey Kripal, a leading scholar of comparative religions, who noted: "paranormal phenomena are semiotic or hermeneutical phenomena in the sense that they signal, symbolize, or speak across a 'gap' between the conscious, socialized ego and an unconscious or superconscious field. It is this gap between two orders of consciousness [...] that demands interpretation and makes any attempt to interpret such events literally look foolish and silly."[94]

The French UFO wave of 1954 involved personal events, where many witnesses reported very strange things, that ran parallel with a social or impersonal dimension that pointed us towards a premonition and warning of an impending collective tragedy. Viewed in this way, it might be possible to propose a richer and more comprehensive interpretation and explanation for the UFO phenomenon.

Could UFO waves be examples of large-scale RSPK? The next three chapters will examine three well-documented cases— the 1952 Washington D.C. UFO wave, the Belgian 1989-1991

UFO wave, and the Rendlesham Forest UFO incident of 1980—
in light of the MPI.

SECTION TWO
Explaining UFO Anomalies

Chapter 4
The 1952 Washington D.C. UFO Wave[95]

The relatively well-documented Washington, D.C., UFO wave of 1952 captured the public's imagination in the early days of the modern UFO phenomenon. In many ways it was a landmark event that shaped the conventional views about UFOs as extraterrestrial spacecraft, as well as fuelling an aura of secrecy and conspiracy surrounding the phenomenon. Yet, very few tried to make sense of it in the broader context of what was happening in 1952. This chapter is a case study and a first attempt to use the Model of Pragmatic Information (MPI) and additional criteria to assess the possible origins of a social psi source for the phenomenon. The Washington D.C. case is relatively circumscribed to a limited number of events, and so the application of the MPI to make sense of what happened is somewhat straightforward.

The July 1952 UFO incidents
Between July 19 and 27, 1952, the city of Washington, D.C., experienced a number of aerial anomalies, or UFO events, which drew considerable attention from the press, the military, and civilian authorities. In particular, the words "flying saucers" were explicitly used by the press to describe these events. Over time, this story became part of the so-called 1952 UFO Wave. Statistically, according to the Project Blue Book database, the 1952 UFO Wave was the largest one in the United States between 1947 and 1969. Project Blue Book was the official UFO data collection effort of the U.S. military that ran, under different names, from the end of 1947 to the end of 1969.

Allen Hynek did a detailed review of all cases submitted to the Blue Book Project from 1947 to 1969. His analysis was based on the 600 or so cases that were considered "unidentified."[96] Of those cases, 242 occurred in 1952, making it the peak year for the period covered by Blue Book. The year 1954 came in a distant second with 46 "unidentified" cases. It is important to note, however, that by the 1960s, Blue Book was much less active and the low numbers for the last few years was clearly an effect of lower reporting rates.

If one pushes the analysis further within the year 1952, the peak month was July with 55 "unidentified" cases, followed by June with 40 cases, August with 28 cases, and September with 27 cases.[97] Hynek did not extend his analysis to cases within the month of July 1952. However, if one uses the National Investigations Committee on Aerial Phenomena (NICAP) compilation of reports, which does not distinguish between "identified" and "unidentified" cases, there were three peaks in July 1952. There was a small peak of sightings on July 12, a second peak between July 21 and 23, and the biggest peak between July 27 and 29.[98] The 1952 sightings occurred across the United States, from the west coast to the east coast, as well as at U.S. military installations in South Korea, Okinawa, Greenland, Newfoundland, West Germany, etc. There were other sightings in 1952 from many parts of the world reported in the press, but these were outside the Project Blue Book recording protocol. The military nature of sightings was also a reporting effect, as military personnel were required to report such observations to Project Blue Book. The events that grabbed the most public attention, however, were two series of sightings that occurred around Washington, D.C., interestingly, just before each of the main peaks for July, namely on the night of July 19-20, and the night of July 26-27. These recurrent UFO events over Washington, D.C., were obvious public events as they were widely reported in the press.

From a sociological perspective, the 1952 UFO wave had some unique characteristics. The wave lasted longer than the previous one in 1947, which was for the most part a summer affair, and got intense but short-lived attention from the press. In April 1952, by contrast, the mainstream and widely read magazine *Life* published a famous article on UFOs, raising both the general awareness about the phenomenon and its respectability. This combination of awareness and temporary respectability certainly had an influence on reporting and can explain in part the higher numbers for 1952, but it cannot account for the relatively high number of "unidentified" cases.

The main source of data used for this case study is Kevin Randle's 2001 book *Invasion Washington: UFOs over the Capitol*. Randle, who is a firm believer in the extraterrestrial hypothesis, produced an extensive chronological study of the July 1952 UFO event near Washington D.C. and it is the most recent and most extensive of such studies available. Strangely enough, Randle's belief in the ETH provides a relative degree of objectivity for anyone trying to understand the UFO phenomenon through a model like the MPI—excluding the possibility of non-human entities as an explanation. For detailed account of the events, please refer to Table 1.

Detailed Chronology of Events

Date	Time	Events
July 19	11:40 pm	**Two radars at ARTC (National Airport) pick up 8 unidentified targets near Andrews AFB.** • Air Controller Edward Nugent notice fast acceleration on radar screen • Sighting confirmed by 2nd radar • Visual sighting by 3rd controller Howard Cocklin (orange ball) • Andrews AFB had nothing on their radar, but visual sighting by William Brady (orange ball) • Brady called others to look but it disappeared very fast • Another military, Bill Goodman saw an orange ball
July 20	01:15	Pilot of flight Capital Airlines 807 saw 7 objects in the sky
	02:00 am	• Tower operator at Boiling AFB saw a "roundish" object, but no radar confirmation • Objects on ARTC's radar, contact Boiling AFB people • Sgt Don Wilson from Boiling AFB saw a white-amber light • Unnamed guard saw an orange color object in the sky • Sgt Charles Davenport at Andrews AFB saw an orange light
	Later	• 3 radars (ARTC, Andrews AFB, Boiling AFB) track an object over Riverdale Radio beacon
	03:00 am	All target disappeared just before 2 jet fighters arrived on the location provided by radar stations
	03:30	Sgt Charles Davenport at Andrews AFB saw an object again
	05:30	• 7 or 8 UFO tracked by ARTC faded away • E.W Chambers saw 5 disks disappearing in the sky [day light]
		Limited interest from military establishment
July 21		Ruppelt, unaware of the events, was on business in Washington D.C., and learn about them in the newspaper, but unable to stay because of red tape
July 26	2:30 pm	Object spotted by Langley AFB radar
	2:50 pm	Second object on Langley AFB radar, but operators thought it might be a weather issue

	8:15 pm	Glowing object saw by crew of a National Airlines plane
	10:30	National Airport, same operators, several spots on radars, confirmed by Andrews AFB. B-25 sent to verify, and always above same point over Potomac River, where a steamboat was cruising
		Number of people on alert given what happen the week before, reporters in the National Airport radar room
	Midnight	2 F-94 sent, one had visual contact with white-blue lights UFO vanished when from radar when F-94 arrived When fighter left, UFO reappeared Another F-94 got lock on, but UFO moved on very quickly
July 27	1:45 am	Jet scrambled again, saw light but could not catch on
	4 to 5 am	Objects disappeared as the sun was rising
July 29		Pentagon press conference, thesis on temperature inversion is presented to explain sightings

The UFO wave and the MPI

The events of 1952, when looked at from a holistic perspective, unfolded in ways similar to a "typical" RSPK event.

Phase One: The Surprise

Von Lucadou describes the first phase in these terms: Generally, the onset of the phenomenon is completely unexpected and the events develop dramatically. As long as those involved believe that the events are due to external factors— someone is fooling them, impulses in electrical circuitry, leaking pipes, etc.—the phenomena become stronger and grow into a real demonstration. Those involved feel ever more insecure and try to find assistance, for example from the police, firemen, or from institutions that can provide technical assistance. In this way the phenomena attract wide attention. In many cases there are a number of respectable, reliable, and independent witnesses, who feel completely perplexed about the causes of the phenomena. This is the "surprise phase."[99]

The first phase of the 1952 events in Washington, D.C., is very similar in its structure to the surprise phase of RSPK events. Around 11:40 PM on July 19, 1952, air controller Edward Nugent at National Airport noticed on the radar screen several strange blips showing a technologically impossible high rate of acceleration, going suddenly from about 120 mph to 7,200 mph.

He called the senior controller, Harry Barnes, to confirm the radar returns. They verified that their equipment was functioning properly. They then asked and got confirmation from a second radar station at the National Airport. As Randle reports: "all the men were puzzled by the events,"[100] and Barnes even confessed later "that the experience of finding unidentified radar and visual targets where there was supposed to be nothing in the air was frightening."[101]

Another controller, Howard Cocklin, saw orange lights in the night sky in the direction where the radar returns were showing up, and commented by saying, "What the hell was that?"[102] Nugent and Barnes sought further confirmation from the radar crew at Andrews Air Force Base (AFB), and although there were no returns, two military men in different locations, William Brady and Bill Goodman, saw orange lights in the sky that they described as taking off "at an unbelievable speed."[103] It is interesting to note that Nugent and Barnes did not know what to think of this event, but they never thought that these returns were "flying saucers" or Russian aircraft, and if they did not appear to be manufactured objects, they seemed nevertheless to be under intelligent control.[104]

Later on, during the night, three different radar stations reported the same strange returns simultaneously. The entire Washington, D.C., area air control system, both civilian and military, came to be on the lookout for UFOs that night. As the phenomenon persisted, the military authorities eventually scrambled F-94 jet fighters, but to no avail; the objects had disappeared.

Phase Two: Displacement
The second phase begins with reporters from newspapers, radio, and television showing up. They give voice to experts who provide the first hunches that something supernatural might be going on. Depending upon the socio-cultural background, the phenomenon may be attributed to phantoms, spirits, the deceased, witches, poltergeists, or other parapsychological forces. Only at this point do parapsychologists have the opportunity to

get involved. Some hunches may have already attributed the phenomenon to one or more persons, and the early feelings of general desperation and anxieties start to fade and get mixed with ones of curiosity: this is the "displacement phase." During this phase, the interpretation of the phenomenon shifts from external to internal sources. The same displacement takes place in the phenomenon itself. New types of events manifest, replacing those that had become familiar.[105]

On July 21, 1952, newspapers were reporting that "flying saucers" were seen in the sky of Washington, D.C., but the coverage was relatively limited. Yet the story was now out and curious journalists were following up on it. During the second set of sightings, on July 26 and 27, there were several journalists in the National Airport radar room.[106] The initial events then repeat themselves in many ways, but with some differences. On the afternoon of July 26 unusual lights were noticed visually and on radar at Langley AFB. Then the crew of an airliner flown by National Airlines saw glowing lights around 8:30 PM. But it was not until 10:30 PM that the National Airport radars returned anything unusual, and the controllers started the process of getting confirmation from other radar stations, as they had the previous weekend.

Once again several F-94 jet fighters were scrambled, and this time, in some occasions, they were able to see strange lights and even briefly have their combat radar locked on them. But then the objects just vanished, though they returned later during the night. Although no one had any confirmation that the objects were solid, as there were only radar returns and visual sightings of nothing more solid than "lights," the press, the next morning, did not hesitate to talk about D.C. being swarmed by "flying saucers."[107] The newspaper headlines were quite explicit in this regard: "'Saucer' Outran Jet, Pilot Reveals," read the banner headline in *The Washington Post*; "Jets Chase D.C. Sky Ghosts," screamed the *New York Daily News*; "Aerial Whatzits Buzz D.C. Again!" shouted the *Washington Daily News*."[108]

Phase Three: Decline

The third phase in von Lucadou's model is the decline of the phenomenon. Journalists hungry for sensationalism and self-appointed "parapsychologists" or "exorcists" will begin harassing those involved. To the external curiosity is added an ever-growing pressure on the initial eyewitnesses to reproduce the phenomenon. The stronger this pressure grows, sometimes even by the parapsychologists who rush to the scene, the less the phenomenon tends to occur: the "decline phase" has begun. Many of those who expected sensational effects are now disappointed and leave. Often the person who evoked the events is accused, sometimes rightly, of fraud during this phase.[109]

This occurred also in the 1952 Washington, D.C., events. The public and even President Truman wanted to be informed about what was going on.[110] The journalists were on the alert for more sightings and information, but no more major events occurred in the Washington, D.C., area, which coincides with the beginning of the overall 1952 wave decline in August. The most significant event of this phase is the July 29 military press conference at the Pentagon, where senior military officials and the director of Project Blue Book, Captain Edward Ruppelt, concluded that it was all a big misunderstanding: the radar returns were most likely caused by temperature inversions, while the lights in the sky were simply stars that appeared to be wobbling because of humidity in the atmosphere. In other words, all the witnesses were mistaken, even those who were experienced technicians and military personnel.

Phase Four: Suppression

Decline is followed by the final phase of poltergeist cases: "suppression." Fraud is more or less openly discussed, the people and witnesses involved are often ridiculed and discriminated in the mass media, witnesses may even deny (in court) their previous statements, and debunking articles are published. The process of social suppression starts.[111] Such conspiracy, however, is not the result of people having secrets to hide, but rather because they do not want to be seen as being ignorant or powerless. As von

Lucadou writes, "neither society nor governmental institutions are fond of the anarchy of poltergeist cases. Their objective is to command (or govern) reliable systems."[112] This last phase of the MPI model should be quite familiar to those who read the UFOlogical literature.

In the case of the post Washington, D.C., events, the suppression was done later on mostly through the efforts of the so-called Robertson Panel, which was assembled by CIA's Office of Scientific Intelligence and which was concerned about the risks of hysteria and panic that could result from a UFO wave like the one that had taken place over Washington, D.C. In early 1953, when the phenomenon had essentially stopped, the panel concluded that 90% of UFO sightings are mistakes or hoaxes, and the ten percent remaining could be accounted for by temperature inversion phenomena and other more exotic natural explanations. The panel also recommended that a mass public education program about UFOs should be put in place so that the U.S. Air Force would not get swamped by reports from civilians. Although the report was classified, several parts of it became public in 1956 when Edward Ruppelt published his book *The Report on Unidentified Flying Objects*. The mass education program was never officially implemented, but the content of the report shows clearly the mindset of senior officials seeking to suppress the phenomenon.

Elusiveness and confirmation

It should also be noted also that the Washington, D.C., incidents are full of examples of the phenomenon ceasing when confirmation became possible, further supporting the usefulness of the MPI when looking at these events. For instance:

1. On the night of July 19-20, 1952, around midnight, airman William Brady at Andrews AFB saw orange lights in the sky. He called his co-workers to have a look. When they arrived, the lights were gone.

2. On July 20, around 3:00 AM, as soon as the F-94 jet fighters could be seen on the ground radar screens, the objects immediately vanished from the radar screens. This scenario was

repeated a number of times during the nights of July 26-27.

3. On the nights of July 26 and 27, F-94 jet fighters lost the objects from their radar screens as soon as they were able to get a lock-on.

4. On both July 20 and 27, the objects disappeared as soon as there was enough sunlight to see them distinctly.[113]

Such elusiveness is very often interpreted as a sign of "intelligent" control, and thus many deduced that UFOs must be spaceships from another world. A similar deductive process occurs in RSPKs and haunting cases where an evil spirit or the soul of a deceased person is "accused" of being the instigator of the phenomenon.

The MPI phases and people

According to the MPI the cast of people involved in an RSPK event display certain similarities. In a "typical" RSPK event, the *environment* is comprised of the people immediately around the *focus person* such as the family, co-workers, neighbors, etc., who collectively do not understand what is going on, and thus, by not focusing tightly on the systems at play, tend to maintain the indeterminacy in such systems during the surprise phase. The *naïve observers* category is comprised of psychics, mediums, and self-appointed parapsychologists who "come to the rescue," as well as sensationalist journalists, and by displacing the interpretation of the phenomenon away from the focus person and onto something "paranormal" they allow the system to remain indeterminate—the displacement phase. The *critical observers* category is comprised of various skeptics, professional parapsychologists, public health officials, etc., who by seeking stringent confirmation reduce the indeterminacy in the system— the decline phase. Finally, the *society* at large, including those in positions of authority as well as the "serious" press, removes any indeterminacy left in the system—the suppression phase.

In the case of the Washington, D.C., events, the *environment* can be clearly identified as the civilian and military aviation personnel, as well as flight crews of civilian jetliners and military fighter pilots. They were key figures in the surprise phase; all of them wondered what was going on. The *naïve observers* were the journalists who congregated in the radar room, and the many "saucer enthusiasts" who read the news reports after the events of July 19-20. They were the key actors during the displacement phase by promoting the views that the anomalies were flying saucers. The *critical observers* were the members of Project Blue Book, Captain Edward Ruppelt in particular, and other technical military personnel represented at the July 29 press conference. Their intervention, which sought a "logical" technical explanation for the anomalies, can be directly linked in a chronological way to the beginning of the decline phase. The *society* was the public, who read the "debunking" news about the Washington, D.C., incidents. They were the central actors of the suppression phase. What is missing, however, is a clearly identifiable *focus person(s)* so that we could understand why a major UFO incident occurred around Washington, D.C., in July 1952, and the meaning behind it (i.e. the content of the pragmatic information).

Who could be the focus persons?
In cases of RSPK the focus person is often but not always someone going through puberty with a lot of unresolved anger. The therapeutic intervention of parapsychologists in such cases is to bring the family to accept that they have unresolved issues and that those issues are at the source of the disturbances. The symbolic meaning that is behind the anomalous phenomenon (i.e. the pragmatic information) can then be expressed by normal means through individual and family therapy and be better understood.

In the case of large scale events, the possibility of therapeutic intervention is not possible, but due to a comparable structure of events one can usually find, after the fact, a critical non-discussed social tension underlying the events. A careful analysis can help us find the identity of the focus persons in large-scale events by using the methodological criteria proposed in the previous chapter.

(1) The Observation System is Social.
The widespread press coverage made it a public event.

(2) Chronological Proximity to a Major Social Event
The Washington, D.C., events, and the peaks of the UFO observation statistics for the 1952 UFO wave, matched closely the timing of the Democratic National Convention that occurred in Chicago, with the unexpected selection of Adlai Stevenson over the favorite, Senator Kefauver, as the Democrats' presidential candidate. The convention spanned July 21 to 26, hence two nights after the first UFO incident and the night before the second one. It is important to note that both Republican and Democratic conventions were televised and covered by three of the four national TV networks of the time. And for the first time ever, half the American population had a TV set to watch it live.[114] And indeed, the UFOs briefly stole show from the Democratic convention on the first page of the *Washington Post* for one July 21 edition of the newspaper.

(3) Geographical Proximity to a Social Group
Following the premises of the MPI, other symbolic clues can be found. The pragmatic information or message appeared to be destined to get the attention of people centered on Washington, D.C. From the perspective of the MPI, it is a good indication that the focus person(s) should be in or around Washington, D.C. As von Lucadou wrote about RSPKs, "Whether he fools his environment or uses psychokinesis, the agent can be assured that all eyes will be on him (or the phenomena) during the surprise phase."[115]

(4) Social Dimension of Symbolism
Another important element is the choice of disturbances. Again, from the point of view of the MPI, the message was conveyed using strange objects in the sky near the capital of a superpower engaged in a Cold War against another superpower, the Soviet Union. It is quite clear that the message was aimed at getting the attention of people in the military. The fact that the phenomenon "persisted" (i.e., lasted two weekends) is also an indication than society at large was another audience for the

message. But as in many RSPK events, the environment did not understand the message. Once again, as von Lucadou asks of RSPK events: "...does the environment understand [the] cry for help? Naïve observers search for all possible causes to 'explain the unexplained,' but they do not recognize its meaning."[116] Instead, aliens in flying saucers and weather inversions are sought for by the naïve observers and the critical observers, respectively.

Finally, as von Lucadou described, there are active and passive RSPKs. The active ones tend to result in the destruction of mundane objects, metaphorically the boiling pot of anger, while the passive ones tend to be expressed via various messages that attract attention to the plight of the depressed individual who cannot speak up. The 1952 Washington, D.C., incidents were certainly not destructive, and imply that we should look for depressed people who were somehow muzzled.

The generic portrait of the focus person, given the available clues, would be someone living near or around Washington, D.C., who felt depressed and muzzled, trying to get the attention of the military, the Democrats, and society in general. The list of potential candidates meeting these criteria can be long, and it is possible to speculate on a number of them, but as with all cases it is not possible to identify a specific person without reasonable doubts. However, if this generic portrait is used to identify a social group as the focus persons, instead of a few individuals, then a different image starts to emerge.

Sociologically, an important contextual element for 1952 was the McCarthy "witch-hunt," which "depressed" and muzzled many in the federal government in Washington, D.C, especially through the loyalty-security program.[117] "McCarthyism and the influence it has exerted are evidence of the deep and anxious apprehension of the American public," Carl Jung noted in his book *Flying Saucers*. "Therefore most of the signs in the skies will be seen in North America."[118]

Furthermore, it is interesting to note that the Democrats, and Stevenson in particular, were enemies of McCarthy, and it was, ultimately, the military that brought McCarthy down by firmly standing up to him in 1954. Thus we have a candidate social group as the "focus person" and the resulting social psi effect.

Overview

The UFO wave over Washington D.C. in 1952 remains an anomalous series of events, within a much larger UFO wave. The controllers at the National Airport had mysterious and disturbing personal experiences with the phenomenon. Yet, how could one make any sense of it without going beyond individual experiences and observations? This chapter has shown that once the individuals' experiences are aggregated into a larger framework, a new perspective emerges.

The events over Washington, D.C., unfolded in ways that are structurally quite similar to a poltergeist disturbance, even if the scale was different; a large metropolitan setting versus a family setting. The structural similarity between these events suggests that the phenomenon could better be explained as a psi-related event. As in traditional paranormal events, the Washington, D.C., UFO wave left no tangible physical traces, and yet something behaved in ways that are unexplainable. It was characterized by a high degree of elusiveness, especially when a possible identification of the phenomenon was nearly at hand. These characteristics are the fundamental features of a paranormal event.

The geography, timing, and symbolism also point towards social anxieties having something to do with the UFO wave, as Carl Jung and others had suspected. The synchronicity of the UFO wave and the events unfolding at the Democratic convention with the resulting political climate in Washington, D.C., is at the very least puzzling. But like any synchronistic event, there is no direct and observable cause and effect between the elements involved. Speculation remains an unavoidable part of dealing with synchronicity. However, when put in the context of structural similarities uncovered through the MPI analysis, the synchronicity between the phenomenon and the social anxieties seems less speculative.

Chapter 5
The Belgian UFO Wave of 1989-1991

The UFO sightings that took place over Belgium in 1989-1991 are probably the best-documented and most significant series of UFO observations that have never had a satisfying explanation. Most of the material gathered on this case is based on the work of a Belgian UFO research organization called SOBEPS (*Société belge d'étude des phénomènes spatiaux*), which enjoyed the substantive collaboration of the Belgian police, and especially, the Belgian military. The SOBEPS produced two volumes of about 500 pages each on what happened and provided various analyses on different aspects of the wave. The data came from 300 audio cassettes (of 60 or 90 minutes each) of witness interviews, 650 investigation reports, and 700 questionnaires filled out by the witnesses.[119]

Although the members of SOBEPS were for the most part seeking to demonstrate the validity of the ETH, their work was very sober and rational, and built on a healthy dose of skepticism. The Belgian military also produced and made public a report, known as the Lamprecht Report, on the UFO chase of March 1990. The report concluded that something real happened but that it could not be explained. This combination of sober UFO research and open support from the authorities makes it an exceptionally interesting case.

Overview of the wave

The "official" starting date of the Belgian UFO wave was November 29, 1989, when Belgian police officers (*gendarmes*) and civilians near the German border observed and reported seeing a strange object in the night sky. There were 143 well-documented observations (125 of them when SOBEPS published its first book in 1991) in the region of Liège that night. From that point on, sightings continued to take place until a spike of 27 sightings took place on March 12, 1991.[120] On December 11,

1989, another spike was recorded with 26 reported sightings,[121] and on the night of March 30-31, 1990, two Belgian Air Force F-16 jet fighters unsuccessfully chased UFOs in the sky. The most intense sighting period overall, however, was between late November 1989 and the end of April 1990.

Histogramme du nombre d'observations de 01.09.89 au 01.12.93

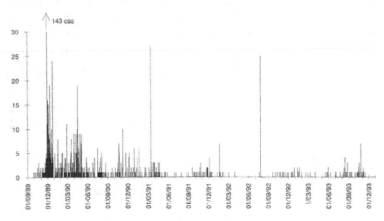

Histogram of Belgian UFO sightings from September 1, 1989 to December 1, 1993[122]

Many sightings involved a dark triangular shaped object with a very bright white light in each corner and a weaker red light in the middle of the triangle. The size of the object was often described as being as large as a jetliner. It should be noted that there were only a few close encounters of the third kind, involving UFO occupants, but they were deemed not credible by the SOBEPS investigators.[123] Only a handful of physical marks were found, potential close encounters of the second kind, but they too were considered by SOBEPS to be inconclusively related to the UFO observations.[124] The bulk of the observations were either close looks at what appeared to be a strange object, or close encounters of the first kind, night lights and daylight discs and other shapes seen at a distance. SOBEPS eventually built up an inventory of over 1,200 cases for that period.[125]

The photographic and video evidence proved disappointing in general, little more than fuzzy lights in the night sky that revealed very little useful information.[126] There was one notable exception, a photo of a dark triangle with white lights in each corner and a red light in the middle that became quite famous in the UFO world, and was the object of many analyses—and much controversy. The photo is known as "Petit-Rechain," named after the locality near Liege where it was allegedly taken on April 4, 1990. But on July 26, 2011, Patrick M. confessed and explained on the French-speaking Belgian television (RTL) how he had hoaxed the picture.[127] Ironically, when SOBEPS investigators were contacted in 1990 to examine the photograph, their first gut reaction was that it is "too good to be true."[128] Indeed, it was.

Key moments of the Belgian UFO wave

It is not possible to cover all the observations made during the Belgian UFO wave of 1989-1991 in a few pages, but here is a synopsis of some of the most impressive events.

The first day: November 29, 1989

November 29, 1989, was the first day of intense UFO sightings in the skies over Belgium. Most of the sightings were concentrated around the city of Liege, but the events started near the German border around the town of Eupen. The first observation occurred around 10:30 AM by a military officer on the ground, who saw a strange and noiseless object that appeared to be flat but about four times bigger than a normal plane.[129] More observations were reported in the afternoon. The witnesses reported a variety of shapes for these objects. In most cases, it was slow or stationary, not very high above the ground, and in all cases noiseless.[130]

At about 5 PM some policemen reported seeing a strange and slow moving object in the sky.[131] About 20 minutes later, two other police officers on a road east of Liege saw a luminous patch about 120 feet in diameter in a field. Then, they saw a flat object in the shape of an elongated triangle with three large lights underneath in a triangular position. They estimated it to be about 90-to-110 feet across at the base, 70 feet in length, and 6 feet thick. The object was at about 375 feet up in the air. It was silent. There was a red rotating light in the middle of the white lights. The police officers were stunned by what they saw. They called dispatch and tried to approach the object with their car. The object stopped, then left abruptly towards the east. The police officers continued driving for a while trying to "discretely" follow the object.[132]

Later, the same two officers went back to their station and asked dispatch to contact the military authorities about possible AWACS electronic surveillance planes in the area, given that there was a major NATO military base in the region. They met with skepticism from their colleagues at first. The military confirmed that there were no AWACS in the area. The officers returned in their vehicle and saw the object again. When they followed it, it stopped and remained in stationary position over a small lake. The red searchlights they saw in the area puzzled the officers. When the searchlights went dim, a red ball of light was "left" where the searchlights were aiming. The red ball went back to the flying object. This happened several times. The officers compared this to a harpoon, thrown away and brought back to its point of origin. The object eventually left around 7:20 PM. They also saw a second triangular object coming out of the first one at very high speed; it had rectangular portholes lit up from the interior and a cupola on top of the triangular base. The second object was also seen by another police officer from the base station.[133]

During the rest of the night, many other witnesses reported strange objects flying in the sky. They included a relatively flat triangular object with powerful lights, a triangular-shaped object with a cupola on the top, a banana-shaped object with portholes, a round shape, an ovoid shape, and a rectangular or lozenge shaped object. The number of lights on the object varied from to two to four, to multiple lights. Some were white and red, in other situations the lights were green, red, and orange. It was noiseless in some circumstances, but produced a humming sound in other occasions. It was stationary, slow, or moving very fast, usually at low altitude. A number of witnesses had a second encounter with the object during that night.[134]

The two police officers who saw the object over the lake were interviewed by a reporter from Belgian television, and the interview was aired the next day on November 30, 1989. On December 1, 1989, most of the French-language Belgian newspapers took up the story as well.[135] By then the UFO wave of observations was a publically known event.

December 11-12, 1989: second spike of observations

That night 26 sightings were reported and subsequently investigated by SOBEPS. It was not as intense as the night of November 29, but there were more objects reported that night than in the period in between. This time the reports came from an east-west axis, starting around Liege, going through the city of Namur, and ending around Mons. The observations all occurred at night, between 5:30 PM and 3 AM. With the exception of two cases, the observations were deemed credible and without obvious explanation by SOBEPS.

Once again, witnesses reported a variety of shapes: a cupola or helmet-shaped object, a triangular object with rounded edges, an elongated triangle, a rectangular shape, and an egg-shaped object. On other occasions, only lights were seen. On some occasions three bright white lights were seen positioned in a triangular shape with a red light in middle, but in other cases, green, yellow, and multi-color lights were noticed too. Again, the object was at times noiseless, while in other situations there was a little vibration noise. It was oftentimes either stationary or slow moving and at low altitude. Several witnesses described the object as being very large, as big as a jetliner.[136]

Probably the most interesting report that night came from Lieutenant-Colonel André Amond of the Belgian Army. At around 6:45 PM, he was driving with his wife to the Gembloux rail station, in the vicinity of Namur. He saw what he called "panels" in the sky with white lights, at the center of which was a red rotating light. He estimated that the panels were 600 to 900 feet up in the sky. He stopped on a hill and observed the object moving slowly for two to four minutes. It was noiseless. The object then turned so that only one light was visible, and it came towards them. His wife became nervous and asked to leave. He too felt the object seemed a bit "aggressive." It was one of the very few cases where the witnesses felt intimidated by the object.

As he started the engine, the bright light disappeared and it was replaced by three lights, not as bright as the first one, and now placed in a triangular position, with a red light in the middle. He estimated the distance between the lights at about 30 feet. Also, he noted that in spite of the full moon, he could not distinguish a particular shape. The object then made a sharp, very slow turn. The white lights disappeared, and only the red one remained until it faded away into the night sky. The total observation time was between five and eight minutes. He noted that the complete silence, the large size of the object, and its slowness were very unusual; he rejected the possibility that it could be a plane or a helicopter. He wrote a report on his experience and sent it to the Belgian Ministry of Defense.[137]

The March 30-31 1990 UFO chase

One of the most publicized aspects of the Belgian UFO wave was the March 30-31, 1990, F-16 chase of an unknown radar return. This event constituted an important part of the Belgian wave, as it generated an array of good quality data from multiple credible sources. Furthermore, this led to increased cooperation between SOBEPS and the Belgian military, in particular, the military officer in charge at the time, Colonel De Brouwer, whose friendly collaboration continued for a number of years afterward.

On March 30, 1990, at about 11 PM, the Belgian police was called by an off-duty police officer, who with his wife and another couple observed some strange lights in formation in the area of Wavre, south of Brussels. It was the odd appearance and behavior of the lights that caught their attention. They were described as moving in an unpredictable way, with lights appearing and disappearing, and changing color, white, blue, red, and green. The witness called the Beauvechain military base south of Brussels. At that point the lights started to move slowly, became almost stationary, and turned red. The witness was told by the desk officer at Beauvechain to contact the Glons NATO radar station instead, about 10 miles north of Liege, as Beauvechain was on minimum weekend manning.[138]

At 11:05 PM, the Belgian military then called the police to get confirmation about the call they received from the witness, and it was indeed corroborated by on-duty police officers.[139] About ten minutes later, two police officers arrived to meet the witnesses. These officers not only saw the lights in the sky themselves, but they also saw two more UFOs with white lights in a triangular formation. When an aircraft passed above the UFOs, the lights moved away from each other and turned red. Once the aircraft passed, the lights resumed their original formation and color.[140] Around the same time, the Glons NATO radar station reported a first return with an unknown.[141]

The police asked by radio at about 11:25 PM if other units could confirm the observations. Two other patrols corroborated the first reports.[142] The military was then informed by the police that they had a total of eight police officers (one off-duty) and three civilians from three different locations confirming the observations. Around 11:50 PM, a second ground radar station further west, at Semmerzake near Ghent, also reported a return from an unknown. At 11:56 PM, the Belgian military decided that it had enough evidence to warrant further investigation, and scrambled two F-16 jet fighters to identify the unknown. Ten minutes later they took off from the Beauvechain airbase.[143]

The UFO chase lasted about an hour in an area midway between Brussels and Mons. Between 12:07 AM and 12:54 AM, the two F-16s attempted nine interceptions. They were able to get three brief radar locks on the objects, in each case causing a swift change in the UFO's behavior. No visual contact was ever made by the pilots. The police on the ground, however, was in constant communication with the Glons radar station and provided them with visual descriptions of what they were seeing from the ground during the chase.[144]

A number of very odd events occurred during the chase. During the first combat radar lock-on, the object went from 150 to 970 knots (170 miles/h to 1130 miles/h) in three seconds, and dropped from 9,000 to 5,000 feet. A few seconds later, it returned to 11,000 feet and quickly went down to ground level. When the second radar lock-on occurred, a jamming signal very briefly appeared on the in-flight screen. At the same time, the police officers and witnesses on the ground saw the lights of the F-16 swirling around in the sky, while most of the UFO lights went off. Finally, unable to identify the unknown, the jets were ordered to return to their base at 1 AM.[145]

After these events, the Belgian military launched an investigation to understand what had happened. This led to the drafting of the Lambrechts Report (named after the author, a Major in the Belgian military).[146] But the Belgian military could not find an explanation to what had happened. In June of the same year the report was released to the public and the Belgian military made all their data available for further analysis by SOBEPS.

March 12-13 1991: third spike of observations

Observations of UFOs in the Belgian skies continued throughout 1990 and early 1991, but at a much reduced rate. During the night of March 12-13, 1991, however, 27 sightings were reported and investigated by SOBEPS. This time the most of the observations occurred near Bierset, a suburb west of Liège, where there is another military airbase.[147]

The observations occurred between 8 and 11 PM. In about one-third of the cases, the witnesses heard a loud noise, while in the other ones the object or lights were silent. The witnesses, given that they were living near a military airport, were all quite familiar with the sounds made by various military airplanes. Yet they reported that what they saw and heard did not match the sound, shape, or behavior of an airplane. Some commentator noted that NATO AWACS re-routed to Bierset might have been responsible for the sightings. But the Belgian Ministry of Defense confirmed that all the AWACS were away in Turkey at the time, as part of a NATO mission to defend that country during the first Gulf War.[148]

Among the strange behaviors reported by the witnesses was the ability of the object to make sharp turns without changing its horizontal alignment with the ground. In some cases, the object was stationary or moving very slowly, and in most cases it had powerful white lights that illuminated the ground. The object's shape was not always visible, but when it was the shape was reported as either being triangular and flat, or circular, or triangular with a cupola on top; variations reminiscent of the observations reported in 1989 and 1990. The objects that were silent were almost all described as either being stationary or very slow and at low altitude. Powerful white lights with a weaker red light were also commonly observed. It was oftentimes described as large as a jetliner. A number of witnesses also reported that they felt as if the object was observing them.

One particularly interesting case that occurred during this period took place in the small locality of Clavier. At around 9:45 PM, a woman and her daughter saw a red-orange ball-shaped light slowly pulsating in the night sky. It was just above tree line, about 30 feet above the witnesses. It moved very slowly, without making any noise, towards the Tihange nuclear power plant a few miles away. A few minutes later, it reached the power plant, turned left, and disappeared in the night. Five minutes later, they saw a large, noiseless, slow, dark, triangular object with flashing lights along its exterior taking the exact same path as the light ball they had seen just moments previously. The following night, the same event repeated itself.[149]

Paranormal aspects

Before looking into the wave as whole to assess whether it unfolded like a large-scale RSPK event, it is useful to point out a number of paranormal aspects of the Belgian wave. Although no credible reports of encounters with UFO occupants emerged from these events, subtle paranormal-related events did occur. As in a classic RSPK, or poltergeist, case, there were a lot of discrepancies in the descriptions provided by the witnesses. As the SOBEPS investigations showed, the UFO reports from the Belgian wave present a rich variety of shapes, colors, and behavior associated with the object. The dark triangle was just one of them. Contrary to what one might expect, there was no consistency in the witness descriptions of the object. As well, some witnesses reported repeated encounters; this is usually noted in UFO events that have a strong paranormal component.

Another interesting feature that is reminiscent of poltergeist events is the object's symbolic behavior. The only substantive observation on the first night came from one of the two police officers near the lake. The object was "behaving" in absurd ways, and gave the impression that it was "fishing for something," or "testing the water," and yet in a hurry (the second UFO leaving the first one at high speed). This symbolism is in the context of a particularly striking feature that people in position of authority, e.g. military officers, police officers, and municipal government officials, were among the very first to witness a strange object in the sky. This suggests an "audience," and even a possible symbolic message: Was someone in a hurry to "test the waters" with the authorities? If the objective of the events was to get the attention of the authorities at large, then it certainly was successful.

Similarly, the events experienced by Lieutenant-Colonel Amond and his wife in December 1989 certainly gave the impression that the attention of the military was being sought. The couple felt that the object was moving towards them "aggressively," or in a determined manner, although there was no violence or threat of any kind. The fact that it happened, once again, to a senior military officer is quite interesting. The famous UFO chase of March 1990 starts again with an off-duty police officer who notices a strange object in the sky, all this leading to a substantive military investigation. Finally, the last peak of reports in March 1991 took place around a military base. Although the observations did not involve many police officers or military personnel this time, they involved people familiar with military aviation, and many reported feeling observed by the object.

Another important point emerging from the various reports collected by SOBEPS is the general practical knowledge that the witnesses had regarding aircraft. Many of them lived near military bases (Glons, Beauchevain, Bierset, and Mons) and were quite used to seeing military aircraft in the sky, such as the large AWACS. Most of them mentioned to the SOBEPS investigators that they thought at first it could be an AWACS, or another military plane, but quickly changed their mind because what they observed in the sky did not match "normal aircraft" appearances and behavior. If the wave had occurred in northern Belgium instead, fewer people would have had practical knowledge about military aircraft. Overall, it seems that the social characteristics of the witnesses were not as random as it might appear. As in RSPK, the phenomenon seemed to select to whom it made itself observable.

The photographic and video evidence produced during the UFO wave is also reminiscent of what many paranormal investigators encounter; strange malfunctions and errors that prevented the witnesses from getting good pictures. Either the picture taken was incorrectly developed, or the camcorder inexplicably failed to record what the witness was filming, or the picture taken showed nothing after being developed, or the film showed an indistinct white light, like a distress flare, or the photograph showed an object so fuzzy that it could be anything you wanted it to be.[150]

One of the most interesting photographic events of the wave happened at Trooz, near Liege, on December 11, 1989. At about 5:45 PM, a family of three adults and the two teenage kids reported seeing what they described as a powerful "searchlight" in front of an object with two other lights at each extremity of a triangular shape that had a row of red lights at the back. The object eventually came right above their house, at an altitude of 150 feet. One adult took three pictures of the object before it quickly moved away. But when the film was developed, it showed only a white vapor on one picture, a trace of something on the second one, and nothing on the third![151]

Even during the UFO chase of March 1990, the much more sophisticated equipment of the Belgian military and NATO personnel produced odd features of the encounter. The Lambrechts Report underlined two particularly interesting aspects of the UFO chase: "Though speeds greater than the sound barrier have been measured several times, not any bang has been noticed. Here also, no explanation can be given," and "though the different ground witnesses have effectively pointed out eight [luminous] points in the sky, the radars have registered only one contact at the same time. The [luminous] points were seen at a distance one from another sufficient for them to be distinguished by the radars also. No plausible explanation can be put forward."[152]

Indeed, the Glons radar station unidentified, seen between about 11:15 PM and 12:20 AM, moved from east to west in a relatively straight line at an average speed of about 25 mph between Brussels and Mons. The Semmerzake radar station confirmed these tracks from Glons.[153] This was quite different from what the F-16 radars recorded. And yet, an interesting feature of the F-16 avionics recording was that it produced a direction for what their radars were sensing but not the distance, as it should normally do. This raised the question as to whether the jets were "chasing" mere electromagnetic perturbations, even though numerous eyewitnesses reported that the F-16s were chasing observable lights.[154] These events seemed to defy laws of physics, just as do various paranormal events. This is also reminiscent of what researchers have found about the interactions between electromagnetism and the human mind.

In a way, these various anomalies are part of the more personal aspects of the UFO wave. Individual witnesses' relationship with the authorities, observations, feelings, problems with equipment, etc., were specific and localized events, and also part of a much larger one. On their own, they seem to make no sense at all. However, once they are combined into a larger framework, a degree of meaningfulness emerges.

The Belgian UFO wave as a large scale RSPK phenomenon

Surprise

As with most RSPK events studied by von Lucadou, the Belgian UFO wave started gently and led to a surprising event. In fact, the first observation of an object similar to what was noted during the wave occurred on September 28, 1989, and was followed by another one the next day. And then, it was followed by nearly a dozen observations until the large peak of sightings on November 29, 1989.[155] However, there is little doubt that the first night of massive observations, November 29, 1989, came as a surprise to everyone. SOPBEPS only realized that something was going on after receiving many calls from witnesses. Those calls came a few days after the events and were sustained in part by the televised interview of the two police officers, and especially the wide press coverage of December 1, 1989. In other words, many witnesses realized that what they saw was a much bigger "event" than they thought, and it was at that point that they decided to report their experience to SOBEPS. Hence, the surprise period could be defined as being from late September to about December 1, 1989.

According to the SOBEPS reports, most witnesses to the events of November 29 did not know what to make of all this. Some speculated that it could be extraterrestrial visitations but did not pursue this interpretation further. All those witnesses, from the point of view of the MPI, constituted the environment of the event, the ones who were surprised; the ones who started to think about non-human entities being responsible for the disturbance.

Displacement

Starting on December 2, 1989, the SOBEPS became actively involved in the events. From the point of view of the MPI, they collectively constitute the naïve observers because, in spite of their rigor and sober approach, they remained committed to proving the Extra-Terrestrial Hypothesis, i.e. ultimately assigning the origin of the phenomenon to non-human entities. New observations were recorded, but at a much lower rate, from zero to half a dozen per day, until the next large observation day of December 11, 1989. There were intense discussions in the press about the UFO wave, especially from December 12th to the18th.[156] On December 18, SOBEPS gave its first press conference, which was well attended by journalists.[157] SOBEPS gave a description of the most common elements emerging from the eyewitness reports.

It is really at this point that the notion of a wave of triangular UFOs takes hold in the social realm.

As previously mentioned, the triangular shape of the UFO

was one among many reported; it was common to just about half of the observations. But by emphasizing the triangular shape, SOBEPS, consciously or not, gave the impression that the observations were more homogeneous than they actually were. In turn, this contributed to creating a collective feeling that a "nuts-and-bolts" ET spaceship visitation was a plausible explanation. The press floated the idea of extraterrestrial visitations, but it remained for the most part relatively objective. The SOBEPS press conference was in many ways a form of displacement, as the ET visitation hypothesis became much more prevalent from that point on.

What is particularly interesting with the Belgian UFO wave is that different social dynamics emerged during the displacement phase, one that differed from what happened during the Washington, D.C., UFO wave of 1952. On December 2, 1989, the authorities, both the police and the military, started their own investigation of the UFO sightings, away from the public spotlight.[158] But four days later, the police approached SOBEPS in order to collaborate with them on the UFO reports.[159] If one reads carefully the SOBEPS book, however, it becomes apparent that the main objective of the police was to "pass the buck" of all their UFO-related work to SOPBEPS, as they were overwhelmed with calls and reports. This attitude is certainly understandable, as the police have limited resources, and dealing with crime, not UFOs, remains its institutional priority. Nevertheless, there was open collaboration with the police.

On December 9, the press reported that the Belgian military was investigating the UFO wave,[160] and on December 15, a military spokesperson confirmed this report in an interview with the press.[161] Then during the December 18 SOBEPS press conference, the Belgian military agreed to send uniformed representatives in support of the SOBEPS investigation. Three days later, the Minister of Defense confirmed in a public statement that they could not explain the unusual sightings that were being reported.[162] Then in January 1990, key SOBEPS members were invited to visit the Glons NATO radar station;[163] by the end of February 1990, an official letter of collaboration with SOBEPS was drafted by the military, and eventually signed a few weeks later.[164]

The active involvement of the authorities constituted a change in pattern when compared with "traditional" RSPK events and the 1952 wave over Washington, D.C. In the usual MPI scenario, the authorities usually try to quell any rumors of unexplainable phenomena. But in the case of the Belgian UFO wave, the response was different. Based on the MPI's logic, if the authorities are supporting the naïve observers instead of reinforcing the actions of the critical observers, then the phenomenon should continue instead of declining sharply.

Decline (?)

The decline phase could be assessed as starting in June 1990, when there were markedly fewer observations on average until the spike of March 1991. The decline was slow, however. It is also during that phase, according to the MPI, that the critical observers usually become active. In the Belgian wave, there were "critical observers" involved early on. The first skeptical attack in the Belgian press occurred on December 8, 1989, and the next day.[165] On December 11, 1989, the hypothesis that an F-117 could be the culprit is discussed in the press, and other skeptical hypotheses about AWACS are presented over the following days.[166] As an interesting synchronicity, on December 19, the United States military invaded Panama, and the F-117 was for the first time publically acknowledged as being part of a military operation. This provided a lot of fuel for the F-117 hypothesis, as the plane's shape and stealth ability could account to some degree for the triangular shape reported by witnesses and the lack of radar tracking at that point. The critical observers made extensive use of the F-117 in their counter-analysis of the Belgian UFO wave. In January 1990, the French popular science magazine *Science & Vie* started what SOBEPS called a "crusade" against the Belgian UFO wave reports.[167] The skeptical attacks continued in the press in spite of the fact that the Belgian Ministry of Defense confirmed that there were no AWACS, stealth U.S. aircraft, or military drones in areas where the UFO reports were coming from.[168] In a curious reversal, it was now the skeptics who did not believe the military version of events.

In spite of the somewhat active presence of critical observers, it appears clear that they could not match the legitimacy that the military authorities gave to SOBEPS by collaborating with them. As noted by von Lucadou in his research on RSPKs, during the Decline phase the phenomenon may try a last ditch effort to get the message across. From that point of view, the last spikes of observations in March 1991 could be construed as just such a last effort.

Suppression (not)

The wave was "officially" considered finished after the March 1991 spike of observations. But in fact there was another spike in July 1992, though the phenomenon was in a way quite different. The object was reported to be uniformly rectangular in shape and having four lights. The sightings were very much concentrated in the south of Liege and had limited connections with the military, other than informing SOBEPS of air traffic in the air at the time. When exactly the wave ended is a matter of interpretation, but it definitely did end—slowly. There was no attempt by the authorities to quell UFO rumors. However, after the release of the Lambrechts Report in June 1990, the Belgian military stopped investigating UFO reports. They limited their activities to providing to SOBEPS, on request, data and verification of air movement. Like most militaries in the world, they "passed the buck" to civilian research organizations, but in a nice way.

Overall, the Belgian UFO wave followed what the MPI would predict for such an event. What was markedly different was the attitude of the authorities, if compared to what usually happens when they are confronted with a RSPK event. But this variation is not unique to the Belgian wave. One can think of situations where haunting stories are actually supported by local authorities, usually when it becomes good for local businesses. This allows the haunting events to continue, and strange experiences continue to be reported. Whether those experiences are self-delusions or psi-related, they do continue. Take for example the American town of Gettysburg, which became one of the most "haunted" places in the world.

What the Washington, D.C., and Belgian flaps have clearly in common, however, is the lack of an obvious focus person that would provide the psi force for the events. Yet, by using an approach similar to the one we used on to the 1952 wave, it is possible to propose possible focus persons that could be at the center of the Belgium wave. In that case, there was a quite obvious social tension involved, although ufologists do not often note it. The "intense" period of the wave, from November 1989 to late spring of 1990, coincides with the fall of the Berlin Wall and the end of communist dictatorships in most of the Warsaw Pact countries. It was the effective end of the Cold War.

The focus persons?

Observation system is social

The first criterion of an observation system that is social, so that social psi effect can occur, is that the wider society needs to be aware that an anomaly is occurring. In the case of the Belgian UFO wave, there are no doubts that it was. The journalist's interview of two police officers who witnessed a UFO was broadcasted on television, and it became a public event almost instantaneously. Then a few days later, the rest of the press was on the story and became even more interested after the second spike of observations of December 11, 1989. SOBEPS and the military were also the center of media interest with the press conference of December 18, 1989. Although the events in Belgium got not only national but international press coverage, the evidence at hand suggests that the phenomenon specifically sought the attention of the police and the military.

Geographical proximity

The second dimension is the geographical proximity, which helps determine towards whom the social psi effect is directed. The UFO wave was very much a Belgian affair. There were only a handful of sightings in the Netherlands, and little if any in

Germany, in spite of the wide media coverage given to the UFO stories. This is particularly relevant because during the first spike in observations there was a widely shared sense that the objects were coming from the east (Germany). During the night of the UFO chase, the radars tracked an object going from east to west.

The observations were concentrated in two areas. One was focused on the area surrounding the city of Liege, and the second was a wide corridor going from the city of Liege to Mons. This geography suggests that the phenomenon was not random either. During the Cold War, Belgium was very much at the heart of the NATO's defense system, but not all parts of Belgium were.

Near Liege was the Glons NATO radar station, which played a critical role in the UFO chase of March 1990. The Glons station was also at the center of the NATO AWACS surveillance system at the time, a key military asset for the Western defense system.[169] And let's note that many thought the UFOs could be AWACS, a specific NATO capability. Note that the UFO "corridor" ends at Mons, where the military headquarters of NATO, known as SHAPE (Supreme Headquarter of Allied Powers in Europe), is located. Finally, the UFO chase of March 1990 occurred almost exactly midway between Mons and Brussels. The political headquarters of NATO is in Brussels. The geographical concentration of the wave suggests that somehow NATO's attention was sought by the phenomenon, not just the Belgian military.

Chronological proximity

One very fascinating aspect of the Belgian UFO wave is how much the documentation about it nearly completely ignored the surrounding world. The UFO wave happened at the same time as the end of the Cold War, which defined the lives of so many people in Europe for over 40 years.

Briefly, Hungary allowed East Germans to leave for the West by opening its borders on September 10, 1989, and Czechoslovakia followed suit on September 30. On October 7, the Hungarian Communist Party dissolved itself. At the end of October, there were massive demonstrations in East Germany, and on November 9, additional crossing points were added on the Berlin Wall, leading to its complete dismantlement. Going through the "Velvet Revolution" and very large demonstrations, the Communist Party of Czechoslovakia also dissolved on November 28. On December 3, the East German leadership resigned, and American president George Bush Sr. and Soviet leader Mikhail Gorbachev declared that the Cold War is over during a summit in Malta. On December 17, Romania went through its own revolution, one marked by violence, and on Christmas Day, the Communist dictator Ceausescu is arrested and executed. Then in 1991, the Soviet Union itself was in trouble. On February 9, Lithuania voted for independence; on March 3, Latvia and Estonia did the same; on March 17, a national referendum was held in the Soviet Union to gather political support for keeping the union together; and yet, on March 31, Georgia voted for independence too.

The second broader contextual element that is also rarely mentioned in connection to the Belgian UFO wave was the UFO wave that occurred in the Soviet Union at the same time. Some researchers did in fact make the connection between the wave and the impending end of the Cold War and of the Soviet Union itself. Jacques Vallée wrote about the USSR wave in 1992 and wondered if the anxieties created by the new policies of Gorbachev could be related to the wave.[169b] An interesting report for the year 1989 was also produced in the USSR, noting that sightings of UFO occupants were relatively prevalent.

The synchronicity between the events surrounding the end of the Cold War, and two concurrent UFO waves, one in the heart of NATO in Belgium and the other in the Soviet Union, is absolutely striking. As noted before, the first sighting of the then "new" triangular UFOs in Belgian skies occurred on September 28, 1989, the day after a strange and odd UFO event occurred in Voronezh in the Soviet Union (where a number of witnesses saw a tall "three-eyed alien" and a robot coming out of craft), and two days before Czechoslovakia allowed East Germans to cross to the West, the final straw that broke the Cold War's back.

The first major spike of observations in Belgium occurred the day after the Czechoslovak communist regime was dismantled and

85

four days before the end of the hard-line East German communist regime. The second spike of observations of December occurred 6 days before the only violent dismantlement of a communist government in Eastern Europe, namely in Romania. The third spike of observations in March 1991 occurred two weeks before the referendum that tried to keep the Soviet Union together.

For those who remember, the events leading to the fall of communism and the removal of the Iron Curtain happened very fast. It was difficult to assess how all this political turmoil would unfold. Hence, there were indeed a lot of social tensions and anxieties in the air in that period. There were worries about a possible military intervention by the Soviet Union to bring the Communist regimes back in line, as happened during the Prague Spring of 1968 in Czechoslovakia. The East German regime was also very hard-line, and its reaction was not clearly predictable and could have led to violent reprisals. The Romanian regime only gave up after several days of fighting between the state security organizations and the armed forces that decided to join the reform movement.

All this suggests the possibility that those who were anxious but could not reach out were the people behind the Iron Curtain during the period of uncertainty. In light of the other criteria, it suggests that they might have been unconsciously trying to reach out, trying to get NATO's attention to protect them from an anticipated bloodbath.

The UFO chase of the end of March 1990, however, stands out as being unrelated to the events of eastern European. By March 1990, the situation was much less stressful, as all the former Warsaw Pact countries had begun transitioning relatively peacefully towards liberal and democratic regimes. April of 1990 marked the beginning of open discussions as to whether NATO had a future in the post-Cold War world.[170] It was a time of flux and uncertainty, but mostly for people who were associated with NATO. The NATO affiliated people were also sharing anxieties about the situation in Eastern Europe and a possible Soviet intervention. The risk of NATO coming to an end and the risk of Soviet intervention in the Baltic States in the spring of 1991 were also very much in the air. If this second line of inquiry makes any sense, then maybe some silent but worried people in NATO contributed to the wave by trying to get the attention of others within NATO.

Symbolic relationship

The symbolism attached to the Belgian wave is also concordant with what the other criteria suggest. The shape that attracted the most attention was the dark triangular object with three bright white lights and a weaker red one in the middle. Using lateral thinking to make sense of this symbolism, two particularly interesting possibilities emerge. The first one is that NATO's symbol is a white star, while a red star usually represented the Communist bloc. The object was often seen as three bright and powerful white lights and a vacillating red light, which symbolically could be a reminder of the weakening Communist bloc being "surrounded" by the more powerful Western bloc. If the pragmatic information was about seeking help from the Western nations, then a message stating "you are more powerful, you can do it" would be meaningful. Another interesting symbolism relates to the elongated dark metal triangles noted by some witnesses. It is very much reminiscent of the well-known NATO's symbol monument at the entrance of its Brussels headquarters.

NATO monument at the entrance of its Brussels Headquarters[171]
Also taking on a new meaning is the report by two police

officers on November 29, 1989, of seeing an object that seemed to be fishing over a lake. The rays were red, and the balls were also red. It is as if the "reds" were fishing or testing the waters. Symbolically, the word "reds" refers to people of the Communist bloc. This suggests that people on the other side of the Iron Curtain were not sure if NATO would intervene and they were "testing the waters" at that time.

Lastly, it's worth pointing out an interesting synchronicity between the events in Belgium, and an event in New York City. In the early hours of November 30, 1989, the Secretary-General of the United Nations Javier Perez de Cuellar was allegedly seen observing a UFO abduction in progress, according to artist and UFO researcher Budd Hopkins. This event was related to Hopkins in April 1991 by a woman who claimed to have been abducted by aliens. Regardless of the truth of the event, however, it is interesting that someone felt compelled to tell an incredible UFO story that involved the one person whose responsibility it was that countries communicate with one another so that events inside the Iron Curtain would not degenerate into an East-West confrontation. It is as if the connections between the UFO events in Belgium and the end of the Cold War were unconsciously established. In any event, it's worth noting that the Belgian UFO wave began its decline in April 1991 just as the events started to become a big story in the media.

So at various levels the Belgian UFO wave seems to be associated with the end of the Cold War, and seemed centered on trying to get the military and NATO's attention. Major spikes in sightings seemed to be interrelated with events to come, as if in anticipation of those events. The end of the Soviet bloc in Eastern Europe occurred very quickly, and although it was something that many people had been hoping for a long time, especially those on the eastern side of the Iron Curtain, the situation was full of unknowns about whether the hardliners would react with force. After all, the hardliners did manage to organize a coup in the Soviet Union in 1992 to bring back "true socialism," and the only reason they failed was that by then the legitimacy of the Soviet regime had been so profoundly undermined, the putsch organizers didn't have enough support to continue.

The Belgian wave, like most UFO incidents, was a mixture of very personal experiences occurring simultaneously with those on a larger and much more impersonal scale. Some Belgian witnesses with whom I contacted personally were clearly changed by the events that happened to them. Their worldviews were changed forever. And yet, they all were left with something that remains beyond explanation, even if some of them have their own interpretation of what it was all about. These personal UFO-related events remain what they are, but they do not prevent the sightings from also having an impersonal dimension that requires a different approach and explanation.

The UFO wave over Belgium was definitely more complex than the one over Washington, D.C., in 1952, even if there are numerous similarities. The odd radar tracking, the military planes chasing the UFOs, and the involvement of the military authorities occurred in both cases. Yet, in spite of the greater complexity of the Belgian wave, it is possible to see that it too unfolded very much according to the MPI hypothesis, once the very different attitude of the military authorities is integrated into the analysis. The Belgian wave also had stranger unexplainable events such as the red balls, the much weirder behavior of the UFOs during the jet fighters' chase, and the strange feelings that witnesses reported. These various elements, once again, are akin to paranormal events like RSPK events, and suggest that they could be a psi-related series of events.

The synchronicity of the Belgian wave with the fall of communism in Europe is striking. The geography, timeline, and symbolisms show a degree of coherence, all pointing towards a call for help to NATO. Yet, like in the synchronicities noted in the Washington, D.C., flap, there was no observable direct cause and effect. Once again, a degree of speculation is unavoidable even if the presence of social anxieties in that part of the world at that time was much more obvious.

Chapter 6
The Rendlesham UFO Incident of 1980

The 1980 Rendlesham Forest UFO incident was not what could be considered a UFO wave. Yet it is well documented and provides enough information to apply the MPI to it in an effort to better understand it. Ultimately it will show that the model can also be used on non-wave events as well.

The famous Rendlesham Forest UFO incident of 1980 appears at first sight to be a relatively straightforward story of military people seeing strange lights and witnessing an odd object on the ground; all of this was documented on paper and on audio tape. But it is, in fact, much more complicated than that. People observed different things during the same event. Statements are somewhat inconsistent, and new information was added later on — at times many years later. Anomalous observations and mundane explanations are difficult to separate in any clean way. This type of fussy and blurry context is actually the norm when one is investigating poltergeist disturbances, or Recurrent Spontaneous Psycho-Kinesis (RSPK). From the perspective of the Model of Pragmatic Information (MPI), such indeterminacy about what is observed and assessed is critical, as it is an important condition for a psi effect to occur. Hence, one could ask if the Rendlesham incident might have been a RSPK event of the UFO kind?

What most people agree on as to what happened at Rendlesham can be summarized as follows.

On the night of December 26, 1980, around 3 AM, two American military security guards, Airman Burroughs and Staff-Sergeant Penniston, while on duty at the edge of the twin Royal Air Force bases of Woodbridge and Bentwaters, northeast of London, separately saw a silent bright light descending into the adjoining Rendlesham Forest. Thinking that it might be a crashed aircraft, they asked permission to investigate beyond the base borders to Duty Officer Lieutenant Buran at base security control. After receiving permission by radio, the patrol was joined by Master-Sergeant Chandler who would stay at the gate with the patrolmen's weapons, as they were not allowed to take them beyond the base. Burroughs and Penniston were also joined by a driver, Airman Cabansag. The three U.S. Air Force personnel then left the base through the East gate and went into the forest where they had seen the strange lights. They drove a short distance and then proceeded on foot. As they moved towards the light, they saw other lights of different colors: blue, red, white, and yellow. They remained in constant communication with the base security control and Sergeant Chandler.

At this point, the story gets a bit more complicated.

Both Burrough and Cabansag related similar events. As they moved closer, they noticed some movement in the woods, and the red and blue lights disappeared. Continuing their march towards the light source, they saw a light that was actually coming from a farmhouse. They also realized after walking for about two miles that a yellow beacon was coming from the lighthouse further away at Orford Ness, by the North Sea shore. At that point, they were told to return to the base. On their way back, a blue light became visible again for a short time. Burrough noted in his report that he could hear lot of noise, sounds like a woman screaming, and agitated farm animals. Cabansag wrote that when they came within 150 to 250 feet of the lights, their radio transmission with the base security became more difficult as there was lots of static.

The report from Penniston is quite different, and unfortunately it was not dated nor signed by him. He noted that he saw a blue light. He also wrote that the three patrolmen were separated by about 30 to 50 feet, and that he could see some mechanical object in the forest, or something of metallic color. He relayed that information to Chandler and Buran, both of whom confirmed receiving Penniston's verbal report about an object in the woods over the radio. Penniston also relayed that there was a lot of noise, and as he got closer the object started to move in a zigzag pattern until he lost sight of it. Both Buran and Chandler noted that somehow Penniston was no longer near the object and could only see the beacon light. After a 45-minute walk, they returned to base.

Both Buran and Chandler essentially stated in their respective reports that they were confident their men had experienced something truly unusual and that the men's judgment was sound and unimpaired.[172]

Later that night, a bit after 4 AM, the military police called the civilian police (Suffolk Constabulary) to investigate the forest, as the area was beyond military jurisdiction. The police investigated shortly after receiving the call and found nothing unusual. The only light visible came from the lighthouse at Orford Ness. In the morning, the military police again called the Suffolk Constabulary about marks on the ground in the area where lights had been seen the night before. They investigated a second time during daylight, and they found three light marks on the ground that could have been made by an animal.[173]

The story then gets even blurrier.

The lights were seen again in Rendlesham Forest on a second night. This time, the information comes from a report dated January 13, 1981, written by the deputy base commander, Lieutenant Colonel Charles Halt. Yet, this report adds a bit of confusion in the whole story. First, the report starts by a recounting the events of the first night (the 26th), but states mistakenly that the first night of events was December 27, 1980. Second, as it discusses the investigation of the 26th, the report states that a metallic and triangular shaped object had been seen, which was two-to-three yards across and about two yards high. As the patrolmen got closer, the object maneuvered and disappeared quickly. This detailed information was not found in any of the reports about the first night. The second paragraph of the report discusses the marks on the ground and relates that later on radiation levels were checked in the area.

Halt's report, in the third and last paragraph, states what happened on the second night, on the 28th: A red sun-like light was seen through the trees. It moved about and pulsed. At one point it appeared to throw off glowing particles and then broke into five separate white objects before they disappeared. Immediately thereafter, three star-like objects were noticed in the sky, two objects to the north and one to the south, all of them about 10°

off the horizon. The objects moved rapidly in sharp angular movements and displayed red, green, and blue lights. The objects to the north appeared to be elliptical through an 8-12 power binocular lens. They then turned into circle-shaped objects and remained in the sky for an hour or more. The object to the south was visible for two or three hours and beamed down a stream of light from time to time. Numerous individuals, including Halt, witnessed these activities.[174]

Years later, through the Freedom of Information Act, the transcript of the 18-minute audio tape made by Lt. Col. Halt during his December 28, 1980, investigation was declassified and made public. Halt had recorded on and off what happened over a period of several hours. Halt went to the site in the early hours of the 28th to investigate the marks left on the ground, after he was made aware of what happened two nights before. It is only later on that night that anomalous lights were seen.

It should be noted that Lt. Col. Halt had problems with some of his electrical equipment. A portable gasoline generator for powerful lights refused to work, and he had to send someone to get another one. They then spent some time taking radiation readings with a Geiger counter where the marks on the ground had appeared. As they were taking the readings, they found what appeared to be marks on trees. Then using night goggles, they found some areas were warmer than the rest, particularly around the marks on the ground. Around 1:48 AM, they heard animal noises from the nearby farm, but researchers later determined that there were no animals at that farm. Halt's attention was then directed to strange lights in the sky. He described the light as red, while others saw it as yellow. The object was described as moving and having pieces shooting off of it. Through their night goggles, it looked dark in the middle, as if it was an eye winking. Other objects appeared and are described in similar ways.

During Halt's investigation, his superior, the American Base Commander Colonel Ted Conrad, was in radio contact with them. Although Conrad and others looked for the lights that Halt was talking about, they could not find them. Some investigators, such as Ian Ridpath, concluded that what Halt and others saw was probably twinkling stars. Others, like Nick Pope in *Open Skies, Closed Minds,* concluded that Halt had a genuine UFO encounter. Halt has given a number of interviews over the years, and some details he provided varied, making the story even more complicated.

The focus of serious debate, however, was the metallic object reported by Penniston to his superiors, Chandler and Buran, and noted in Halt's report. Penniston wrote that he was about 150 feet away when he saw the object at night in a forested area. Furthermore, not only is Penniston's report unsigned and undated, but there is more detailed information in Halt's report than in Penniston's report. That's puzzling because Halt was not present the first night. Basically there seems to have been only one witness to the object in the woods, making this part of the story more difficult to assess. Several years later, in 1994, Penniston decided to undergo hypnotic regression, during which he "revealed" more details about the "craft" he saw in the forest. It was reported that, "Under hypnosis, Penniston describes the alien visitors, saying that they are 'travelers from our future.' They have been coming here in teams; each team assigned a different 'tasking,' a different mission. Each team targets certain people when it comes back to our time, rather than just encountering people randomly."[175] One of the interesting aspects of the regression was his "recollection" of seeing symbols on the craft. More on this later.

After the events of December 1980, reports were sent to the UK Ministry of Defence (MoD), but nothing of substance occurred afterward as the incident was not thought to constitute a threat to national security.[176] Researcher David Clark has noted that "Nevertheless, within months of the incident in January 1981, rumours about a UFO landing at the base leaked out to civilian ufologists, along with a story that an unidentified object had been tracked by RAF radars. During 1982 when the protest against American Cruise missiles at RAF Greenham Common was underway, the MoD began to receive letters asking if the UFO story had been spread to conceal a military accident involving a missile or aircraft."[177]

As information became more public, the debate intensified

on numerous issues. There was apparently radar tracking of something unusual for those nights, but after investigations other much more mundane possibilities to explain them were put forward. The radiation levels found at the site were considered normal for the type of instrument used by Halt's crew. There was a Soviet satellite in re-entry at the time of the events, but not at the exact time. There was allegedly a covert U.S. Air Force security investigation of the events, but there has been no trace of it, and no confirmatory witnesses. The marks on the ground were likely made by animals, likewise for the marks found on the trees, or maybe they were the result of other trees falling on them, etc. In the end, the Rendlesham incident is either the "British Roswell," the "best documented" UFO event on British soil, or "much ado about nothing," depending on your point of view.

The Rendlesham incident from a different perspective

The Rendlesham incident seems to have unfolded just as the MPI proposes for poltergeist events. The events of the night of December 26 were the *surprise phase*. Something odd occurred and people start investigating. At first they thought that it might be an aircraft that crashed. But a closer investigation presented strange lights and strange goings-on in the forest. As they came closer to confirmation, the anomalies ceased and the mundane light coming from the lighthouse was all that was left. The three patrolmen and their superiors can be viewed as being the ones making up the Environment; the first ones to be aware that something odd was happening given their normal security duties. The patrolmen did not know what to make of this, but it was for them clearly an unusual event. Penniston claimed to have a seen a craft. Whether this was an accurate description or an illusion, it seems clear that he started to formulate a hypothesis about what happened. And as in a classic RSPK event, they called the police for assistance, but to no avail.

The *displacement phase* occurred the day after through the involvement of Lt. Col. Halt. The phenomenon occurred again, but in a different way, with only lights in the sky on the 28th. In this sense, it was different from the night of the 26th because nothing anomalous happened in the forest itself; it was all in the sky. Halt's focus was clearly on the marks on the ground; he was looking for potential radiation. He made note of the marks on the trees and the warm spots on the ground. His report, emphasizing and augmenting Penniston's report about a metallic object, reinforces the notion that Halt was looking for a physical object in the area. Finally, based on the various interviews he gave over the years, it appears that Halt believed that some physical object had landed in the forest. Halt, in many ways, displaced the attention from lights in the sky towards the ground. Using von Lucadou's terminology, his behavior and attitude fits the profile of the "naïve observer," even if he was not necessarily naïve during the events. It was during his presence that the phenomenon was actually the most intense and had the greater number of witnesses. Note that Penniston and Burroughs appear to have had no substantive involvement during the second night of observations.

The *decline phase* occurred during the latter part of the events of the 28th. Halt was in constant radio contact with his superior, Col. Conrad. Conrad and the people with him decided to go outside to look for the objects described by Halt, but to no avail; they could not see them. It was more or less at this point that the objects became "less interesting" and eventually "boring" enough for Halt and his men to return to base. Conrad can certainly be described as a critical observer, and as in a "typical" RSPK event, this type of observer tends not to see or hear anything odd, and the phenomenon ceases relatively quickly after their involvement. Conrad has given a few interviews over the years; he thought that Halt had embellished the story.[178]

The *suppression* phase occurred as the reports were funneled to the British Ministry of Defence (MoD), namely the authority representing society in von Lucadou's model. The MoD did suppress the issue. Once they were satisfied that the events did not constitute a threat to national security, they closed the file on the case.

These events vary somewhat from the traditional RSPK event in that they occurred within the U.S. military and by extension the British MoD, both of whom are members of the authority.

Hence, the actors could only come from within that organization, instead of being the usual neighbors, self-declared psychics, or the skeptic debunkers. These others eventually became involved, but only years after the events, when the events became known outside the military.

Paranormal aspects

Every time the field where the events took place was investigated, the patrols experienced challenges with electrical equipment. The radio was not working well the first night, and the lighting power generator refused to work during the second night. Problems with electrical equipment are a common feature of RSPK events.

Then, during both investigations, strange and loud noises were heard, once resembling a woman screaming, and agitated farm animals on both occasions. Yet, as we know, the nearby farm had no animals. Others have suggested that the noises could have come from animals in the forest, but this seems an unlikely explanation. When humans talk in the forest, animals tend to hide and stay away; this is especially true in the middle of winter. RSPK and UFO events, on the other hand, are filled with accounts of unexplainable noises and voices.

During the first night, the light seemed to be "playing" with the patrol. As soon as they came close, it seemed to move away. This eventually mutated into chasing a mundane light, the Orford Ness lighthouse. This playful aspect is a common feature of RSPK events; something seems anomalous at first but later it is not, such as a knock on the door with no one there, but a few minutes later someone who is not known for doing pranks knocks on the door for real.

Lastly, as is typical in RSPK stories, the witnesses reported seeing different things during the same event, Penniston versus Burroughs and Cabansag on the first night, and Halt and his team versus Conrad and his crew on the second night. Psi phenomena are not completely subjective, and yet not completely objective either. To classify such events as one or the other will make us miss the reality: these are essentially hybrid phenomena.

The focus person?

Once again, we have a situation where events have a personal impact on people, especially Halt and Penniston whose lives became deeply intertwined with this UFO incident. Also, Burrough, now a veteran, claimed and received in 2015 medical compensation for disabilities caused by unhealthy exposures during his military service. The accepted claim includes a mention of the Rendlesham events as a contributing factor,[179] based on a MoD report speculating that people at Rendlesham might have been exposed to intense but not ionizing radiation.[180] And yet, we have also an impersonal event that extends much beyond the individuals involved.

In a classic RSPK case, a person at the center of the events would be under substantial psychological stress and yet be unable to communicate that distress for some reason. The psychokinetic effects become an alternative way to communicate this need for help. If the Rendlesham forest incident is something akin to a RSPK disturbance, then who would be the focus person? Who is seeking help?

The first feature to look at is the *observation system*. There is no social observation system in the case of Rendlesham in that it was not a public event when it unfolded, even if it became one in the years to come. But neither was the observation system an individual one. The people whose attention was sought by the phenomenon were clearly the military authorities. This incident made its way, eventually, to the highest echelons of the defense establishment in the United Kingdom. There were also two countries involved, as the bases where it occurred were in the UK, but the personnel and aircrafts were American. Finally, those bases had nuclear capable forces, and the squadrons were deployed in the context of the Cold War. So, it can be said that, indirectly, the observation *was* social.

The second set of clues we need to look for is the *geographical proximity*. If there was a message, or pragmatic information, to be sent to the military authorities, why was it at Woodbridge/Bentwaters? At first sight, there seems to be nothing really particular about these bases. Yet the area was also the site of another military establishment: the British Atomic Weapons Research Establishment (AWRE) at Orford Ness, which was situated very close to the lighthouse. The labs had stopped operating in 1971, and the research center was closed in 1973.[181] When it operated, it was used mainly to assess the environmental soundness and functional performance of various parts of the atomic bombs developed by the UK.[182] However, in 1980 its powerful medium-wave transmitting station was still being used by the Foreign Office.

The *chronological proximity* is the next clue. What happened in December 1980 that could trigger a RSPK-like event? Again, nothing obvious shows up at first. In the 1980s, the Americans seriously considered deploying nuclear armed cruise missiles in the UK, and the British government consented to it. In July 1980 Secretary of State for Defence Francis Pym told the House of Commons that a total of 160 Cruise missiles would be located at RAF Greenham Common, Berkshire, as well as the disused RAF Molesworth in Cambridgeshire.[183] This was in response to the deployment of medium-range Soviet missiles, all of which became known as the Euro-missile crisis of the 1980s. Many consider this time period nearly as dangerous for a nuclear confrontation as the Cuban missile crisis had been two decades earlier.

As divulged in an article published in *New Scientist* in 2007, the AWRE published two classified reports on the safety of the potential deployment of American nuclear warheads at Greenham Common. The second report was dated December 2, 1980, and the report stated: "If one warhead were to detonate it is possible that the other seven warheads in the storage cell could be engulfed in the fire which is virtually certain to ensue from the rupture of the missiles' fuel tanks."[184] These British reports relied heavily on American data and research, and focused mainly on potential plutonium pollution. To justify why they engaged in further research, the report states: "It was assumed at that time, on the basis of US assurances, that accidental detonation of the [blacked out] in one or more of the [blacked out] warheads is impossible…"[185] Ironically, the AWRE was also at the same time dealing with plutonium pollution of its own, which had been discovered in 1978 at their main installation in Aldermaston and had seriously affected several employees, which led to a formal investigation by Sir Edward Pochin. The AWRE refused to take much responsibility for what had happened to those unfortunate employees.[186] By December 1980, the AWRE was still trying to find ways to improve safety. According to the Redfern Inquiry launched in 2007, the AWE, the new name of AWRE, had the same attitude of taking as little responsibility as possible for what had happened.[187]

The last set of clues to look for is at the *symbolic level*. On the first night of the encounter, the phenomenon seemed to be "playing" with the observers and leading the American military personnel to Orford Ness. On the second night, the phenomenon seemed to instruct the American soldiers to stop looking at the ground and look up instead. There were noises sounding like the screaming of a woman, symbolically representing distress.

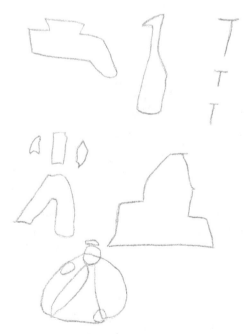

Reproduction by the author of Penniston's notepad drawings[189]

Another symbolic clue, which many people discounted, involved the symbols that Penniston drew after going into hypnotic regression in 1994. It is well known that such regression can produce false memories and made-up events, but psychotherapists using hypnotic regression have also noted that people have visionary experiences in such circumstances that could involve ESP.[188] The information gathered in such a way is very rarely clear, and it is usually symbolic with bits and pieces of more objective information embedded in the vision. Penniston made drawings of them, and on page 101 they are reproduced in a similar hand.

If we compare these images with the symbols on an iconic monument of the anti-nuclear movement in the UK, interesting parallels emerge. By 1983, Greenham Common became the site of a primarily female organization's permanent demonstration against the nuclear weapons. The women eventually produced a collective quilt that became emblematic of their struggle to get the weapons removed from the base. This quilt was reproduced as a monument where the demonstration occurred. A picture of it is shown below:

Monument reproducing a collective quilt designed by anti-nuclear protesters of the 1980s at Greenham Common[190]

A close up on some of those squares present interesting connections with what Penniston claims to have seen:

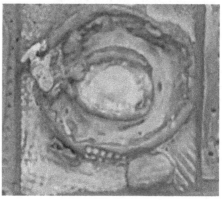

Detail of elements of the Greenham Common Quilt monument

Finally, as noted previously, by 1982 many letters were sent to the MoD in the context of a growing anti-nuclear demonstration at Greenham Common, asking if the UFO story was a cover-up for a crashed plane. The events of Rendlesham and the political crisis surrounding the nuclear weapons at Greenham Common seemed somehow linked. Was this social psi in action?

In light of all these elements, it would be reasonable to think that one or more persons at the AWRE, maybe former employees of the Orford Ness lab (as they were moved to Aldermaston after the closure),[191] became very concerned about the upcoming deployment of the American nuclear warheads, as well as being disgruntled about how the AWRE was managing its own plutonium pollution. The study conducted and reported in the

AWRE document of December 2, 1980, required the precise expertise that could be found among those who worked at Orford Ness before its closure. The report was at the time classified as Secret ATOMIC CONIFER,[192] so the focus person(s) would have been completely muzzled about it. Could that person have been visiting old friends at the Orford village during the Christmas season of 1980, as it continued to be the residence of many ex-employees of the research center who became employed with the British government in the nearby town of Martlesham?[193] As in the previous cases, it is quite hard to pinpoint precisely the potential focus person(s) of an impersonal UFO event, but the connection Greenham Common/Aldermaston/Orford Ness is certainly an interesting one.

The PK/UFO effects then would have been an alternate way of communicating with the American military authorities about the danger of such deployment. In a way, the message was partially understood, but not until many years later in 2001 when Admiral Lord Hill-Norton, the former Chief of the UK Defence Staff, famously stated that such an incident near a nuclear base should be taken seriously.

Lastly, and once again, it is also possible to think that there might have been a parallel "layer" of social psi force engaged simultaneously with the Rendlesham Forest events. The well-known UFO encounter that eventually became known as the Cash-Landrum Incident, based on the name of the people who were involved, Betty Cash, Vickie Landrum, and Colby Landrum, occurred on December 29, 1980, in Dayton, Texas, near Houston. This was the day after the second event in the Rendlesham Forest. A key feature of the Cash-Landrum incident was that the witnesses suffered from an unexplainable illness, whose symptoms looked to some people very much like radiation poisoning.

It has been often reported that Betty Cash's doctor, Dr. Brian McClelland, told the *Houston Post* in September 1991 that her illness was a "textbook case" of radiation poisoning, and thus implying exposure to ionizing radioactive elements like the radiation produced by uranium or plutonium (i.e. highly energized particles that can go through matter). However, a closer look shows a more complex image; it's as if the symptoms of ionizing radiation poisoning were actually mimicked. Researcher Brad Sparks and Dr. Richard Niemtzow, who investigated the case of the behalf of APRO, noted that the witnesses' symptoms were more in line with chemical agent poisoning. Some chemical agents can mimic ionizing radiation poisoning.[194] Severe burns on the skin, vomiting, and nausea shortly after exposure can indeed be interpreted as acute radiation syndrome.[195] However, acute radiation syndrome is also a sign of exposure to high levels of ionizing radiation, usually fatal within a few days or a few weeks.[196] But non-ionizing radiation at very high levels, such as microwave, intense radio frequency emissions, and very strong magnetic fields can also cause nausea and skin burn but is not lethal.[197] Keeping in mind the important role that electromagnetism plays in the UFO experience, this alternative approach provides a different interpretation to these events. It goes without saying that the timing and the symbolism of these events present a curious synchronicity to the Rendlesham Forest incidents.

The Rendlesham Forest incident, even if it was a relatively self-contained series of two observations of lights in the sky, was still a complex event. It unfolded very much like a RSPK event, except that it happened within the social realm of people in position of authority. This may explain why it did not last long in spite of the potentially strong social psi force that could have emanated from fears of a nuclear holocaust.

SECTION THREE
Complex UFO Encounters

Chapter 7
The Canadian UFO Wave of 1966-1967

Continuing our analysis of cases of greater complexity, we will next turn our attention to a series of events that took place in Canada in 1966-1967, which was not recognized as a "wave" until after the fact. For instance, Canadian researcher John Magor wrote an article in 1969 entitled "1967 Canadian UFO Wave: The Year We Were Invaded Without Knowing It."[198] Magor noted that people in Canada were aware that something was going on in the sky, but they did not really grasp the magnitude of the events.

This wave was actually part of a much larger, but diffuse, wave that also affected the United States. Once looked at as a whole it was an impressive UFO wave. Some ufologists have hailed the 1966-1967 UFO wave as the "mother of all UFO waves."[199] Yet, as in Canada, it was also a less obvious one. John Keel was one of the few who wrote about the 1966-1967 UFO wave as it was unfolding.[200] But for many, the full realization that a major UFO wave was happening came afterward, as was noted by the late Richard Hall during a 1978 MUFON conference.[201]

But for the sake of providing a more manageable illustration here, we will focus only on the Canadian sub-set of the 1966-1967 UFO wave. If compared to the cases studied in the previous chapters this wave is definitely a more diffuse and subtle series of events than the 1952 Washington, D.C., the 1989-1991 Belgium wave, and the 1980 Rendlesham incident. In a way, if well-circumscribed UFO waves can be studied as poltergeist events, diffused and subtle UFO waves are more like hauntings with less spectacular but longer lasting anomalistic incidents. In such cases, I've found the four-step MPI to be less useful, and I will therefore introduce other conceptual tools to help us understand the phenomena.

UFOs and Morphic Resonance
Rupert Sheldrake, a biologist, has proposed the concept of morphic resonance to describe the propagation of information

in the universe. He applied his concept not only to explain how similar biological information tends to spread in the living realm, like having symmetrical forms (two eyes, two arms, two legs, etc.), but to psi as well. Whether the psi is of the ESP or PK kind, it can be understood as acquiring or modifying information. The concept of morphic resonance is therefore very much amenable to an understanding of psi events.

So what exactly is morphic resonance?

Sheldrake explains: "All self-organizing systems are wholes made up of parts, which are themselves wholes at a lower level, such as atoms in molecules and molecules in crystals. The same is true for organelles in cells, cells in tissues, tissues in organs, organs in organisms, organisms in social groups. At each level, the morphic field gives each whole its characteristic properties, and interconnects and coordinates the constituent parts. The fields responsible for the development and maintenance of bodily form in plants and animals are called morphogenetic fields. In animals, the organization of behaviour and mental activity depends on behavioural and mental fields. The organization of societies and cultures depends on social and cultural fields. All these kinds of fields are morphic fields."[202]

In other words, what exists at small scale is reproduced at the larger scale, but without being reducible to one another. For example, individuals can be angry, just as a crowd can be angry. But a collection of angry individuals does not make an angry crowd; they need something that stimulates their collective anger, like a crowd organizer. Conversely, in an angry crowd not everybody is angry and some will of their own choosing try to stop the angry ones. So human emotions can be seen as a field playing at more than one level, but it can "resonate" from one level to the next, from the individual to the crowd and vice versa.

RSPK events can be understood in terms of morphic resonance. The focus person's challenges are an emotional and symbolic field that resonates into the physical field through poltergeist disturbances, or PK effects, as well as through ESP effects. From that point of view, the MPI does not contradict the notion of morphic resonance; rather it is a particular case of morphic resonance. In the same vein, many people explain hauntings as emotions and symbolic communication somehow stuck in time, but resonating into the present mental fields of living people and to a lesser extent into physical fields. If UFO events are psi and social psi related, then they could also be construed as due to some morphic resonance occurring between individual psi and social psi fields, as well as between mental and physical fields through PK. Morphic resonance offers less granularity for analyzing UFO cases than the MPI, but it is still helpful in making sense of events.

The 1966-1967 wave

One important difference in the Canadian wave of 1966-1967 is the changing nature of the "observation system," i.e., how UFO incidents were reported. Governments in North America in the 1960s came to suffer from "UFO fatigue." By 1966 Project Blue Book was but a shadow of former self, and the USAF was looking for a way to unload its responsibilities, which it ultimately did after the University of Colorado Condon Report said that UFOs were not worth spending any more time on. In Canada, National Defence finally transferred their UFO files to the National Research Council in September 1967,[203] who passed the buck to a group of University of Toronto professors to create a Canadian version of the Condon Committee. Hence, the "observation system" was in transition from a "public" governmental overview to multiple and oftentimes unconnected "private" UFO organizations taking over the recording of the events.

The ultimate outcome of all this is that the recording of events and overview came to rely solely on private citizens organized in UFO clubs and associations such APRO, NICAP, CAPIC and many others. By the 1970s, the observational system essentially became privatized (i.e. outside the realm of governmental authorities) and very fragmented across many UFO groups.

From the parapsychological point of view, this is a very important issue. As noted previously, psi effects are the outcome of human will to affect unconsciously desired intents through non-normal means. Social psi works in similar ways, but represents a collective unconscious desire instead of an individual one. Psi and social psi represent alternative attempts to express emotionally charged messages. Changing who could actually be aware of the psi effects or anomalies also changes how psi could be used to reach an unconsciously intended audience. Hence, in the mid to late 1960s the UFO-related emotions that would be carried through psi and social psi effects would reach less and less the public authorities and society at large and only reach a limited number of local people through various private and disjointed UFO groups. In other words, the potential recipient of the intended messages was changing, and therefore the nature of the message would change also.

Anatomy of a diffuse UFO Wave
The data set for this case study was produced by combining Richard Hall's study of the 1966-67 wave,[204] the Government of Canada Archives,[205] and the websites UFO DNA[206] and Water-UFO.[207] The choice of these databases was based on their apparent comprehensiveness, their identification of sources, and how systematic they were in coding the data. About a dozen sightings were not included, as they were either explainable by conventional means, or not enough information to make any judgment.

   The overall results are as follows:
Total sightings for 1966: 122
Total sightings for 1967: 233
Total for 1966-1967: 355

   As it is the case for the vast majority of UFO sighting reports, there is very little information to work with. The impact on the witnesses was rarely recorded unless there are physiological effects or very ostentatious psychological impacts. Given these circumstances, it is impossible to assess a potential psi effect for every case except for those few that were investigated in greater depth, such as the Falcon Lake incident. This is a limitation found in the vast majority of the UFOlogical material. However, basic statistical trends may be useful to assess if something was occurring above the level of the individual witnesses; namely, were there some impersonal forces at play too?

A first general finding of this case study is that the 1966-67 UFO wave in Canada had a relatively high percentage of "unexplained" cases. This is in line with the Hynek study of the 1952 UFO wave, and the SOBEPS study about the Belgian wave. In other words, a key characteristic of a UFO wave is not only having more sightings but also having a greater percentage of "unexplained" cases.

Since with historical cases, it is impractical to investigate properly all the unexplaineds, one has to focus on those that present the best evidence that something truly unusual has happened, which in the UFO world tends to be those known as close encounters (CE), as Hynek classified them.[208] Once the cases are limited to the CEs, the Canadian data is as follows:

Year	CE1	CE2	CE3	Total	% of cases
1966	29	7	2	38	31.15
1967	53	25	11	89	38.20
Total	**82**	**32**	**13**	**127**	**35.77**

Close encounters constitute nearly 36 percent of all cases. Even if only one-third would still remain unexplained, had there been a substantive investigation for each of those cases, there would still be about 12 percent "unexplained."

In light of these CE cases, some patterns start to emerge. The wave was diffuse over two years, and it occurred across the country. But if one focuses only on the close encounter cases, then six particular clusters of sightings emerge. These clusters are:

(a) Concentration of nearly half (15 out of 38) of the close encounters over the early summer of 1966 (between 1 June and 8 August), with a concentration in the last week of July. In this case, both the government (the public observation system) and private UFO organizations (the private observation system) were "looking" into these events, as their respective reporting system produced reports for this cluster.

(b) The Hamilton/Caledonia area in Ontario experienced a mini wave of its own in January and February 1967, with a short but intense second outburst in June 1967 (including a prominent CE3 experience, and one of the rare Canadian "men-in-black" reports). This was essentially noted by the private UFO organizations (i.e. the private observation system).

(c) The Sudbury area, also in Ontario, experienced a mini wave between September and November 1967, with an interesting sighting on October 4, the day of the Shag Harbour incident. Only the government looked into details of these Sudbury events (the public observation system).

(d) At the end of July and August 1967, there was a concentration of CE3 experiences (6 of 13); almost half of all CE3 reports for the entire UFO wave. In this case, only private UFO organization paid serious attention to these events (private observation system).

(e) The Shag Harbour incident is also noteworthy because of the simultaneous high quality sightings in Sudbury and in Quebec, as well as a very interesting case from Nova Scotia sharing many similarities with a RSPK event. In this case, substantive reporting was produced by the government and private UFO organizations (i.e. both the public and private observation systems were on the lookout).

(f) The famous Falcon Lake incident of May 20, 1967, appears to be a geographically isolated incident. But a closer look reveals that it is located within a cluster of 12 close encounters between late April and late May 1967 (or about ten percent of all close encounters for the entire wave). This cluster was essentially reported on by private UFO organizations (the private observation system).

UFO clusters in Canada in 1966

The Canadian public observation system was already in place in 1947, as there were UFO reports produced by the Royal Canadian Mounted Police (RCMP) and the Department of National Defence (DND). The first attempt to provide a wider overview of the phenomenon was a "one-man" authorized initiative, known as Project Magnet, led by Wilbert Smith, a civil servant, in the 1950s. Smith became a firm believer that UFOs were of extraterrestrial origins, but his project was shut down for lack of evidence. Smith, however, was allowed to use government scientific equipment to continue his investigation outside work hours. (He passed away in 1962.) A parallel project called Second Storey was created by a mixed group of scientists and military personnel to review UFO cases in government hands. This project did not lead to any substantive conclusion about the nature of the UFO phenomenon, other than it was no threat to national security, and the project was also shut down.[209]

By the 1960s, the public observation system was not unified, as reports were received by a number of different agencies like the RCMP, DND, National Research Council (NRC), and the Department of Transportation (DOT, now known as Transport Canada). The formal transfer of files from DND to the NRC, and the enrolment of University of Toronto professors to study the phenomenon in 1967, led to as close as it could be to a unified public overview of the UFO phenomenon. This has never been the case in Canada since.

Yet the UFO phenomenon attracted the attention of some important public figures. On April 5, 1966, in a now declassified Cabinet memorandum, Prime Minister Pearson asked to be briefed on the UFO phenomenon given the "interest shown in Parliament."[210] If the intention of the phenomenon was to attract the attention of the authorities and by extension society in general, it succeeded.

The Maritime mini UFO wave of summer 1966

The first observable concentration of UFO reports occurred in the Maritime Provinces, namely New Brunswick, Nova Scotia, and Prince Edward Island in 1966 between June 16 and August 8, at a time when the Prime Minister of Canada had shown an interested in UFOs. The first difficult to explain event occurred on July 22 near Fredericton, New Brunswick, and was described by some as a ball of light, and by others as a stationary triangular object.[211] The second occurred on the same date over Halifax, Nova Scotia, and was described as a cigar by some and as a triangle at low altitude by others. No helicopters were flying in the area.[212] These events occurred in urban areas and got the police involved, which in turn informed the RCMP. Interestingly, these descriptions are reminiscent of what witnesses reported during the Belgian UFO wave. On July 28 there was also a sighting at Summerside Canadian Forces Base, which attracted the military into looking into these events.[213]

If indeed this was an event with a psi component, then the next question would be to ask if there was a symbolic message associated with it. The fact that the UFO events occurred in areas which at that time would attract the attention of the authorities can imply that a message was aimed at the authorities, i.e. the public observation system. If so, what could have been the possible symbolic message conveyed?

It is interesting to note that both sightings of objects said to be triangular in shape occurred on July 22 near the provincial capitals of both provinces involved: Fredericton in New Brunswick, and Halifax in Nova Scotia. This provides an interesting clue about the possible political nature of the symbolic message for the politicians. To learn more requires some in-depth research on the local situation at the time, and about possible local social anxieties, which are usually not discussed publicly.

One possibility centers on the identity tensions around the rise of official bilingualism (English and French) in Canada. As will be discussed later, Canada at time was going through a substantial uptick of tensions between the French-speaking minority and the English-speaking majority. Prime Minister Pearson's expression of interest in UFOs in the Cabinet occurred the day before his announcement in the Parliament of April 6, 1966, that the Canadian government should be officially bilingual. New

Brunswick eventually became officially bilingual, while Nova Scotia resisted making accommodations to the French-speaking Acadians for quite some time. Could these triangular UFOs have been indicative of morphic resonance, pointing the linguistic arrow in a different direction?

The British Columbia mini UFO wave of summer 1966

Around the same time as the Maritime mini wave was another one that occurred in British Columbia (BC) at the other end of this vast country. But this cluster of close encounters in the summer of 1966 was essentially observed by the private system, namely by citizen-based UFO organizations. At a more general level, however, this synchronicity of observations between the East and West coasts is interesting, as it gives an impression of a "coast-to-coast" message. "Coast-to-coast" is Canada's official motto, written in Latin on Canada's Coat of Arms.

The BC cluster includes a CE3 event that occurred in Qualicum Beach on Vancouver Island in July 1966. A witness stated that entities illuminated him with powerful lights, but caused no other effect, and then vanished. On July 30, the NRC (the public observation system) received one report of a metallic grey circular object in Richmond, just south of Vancouver. On August 2, two independent witnesses reported seeing a disc-shaped object up-close in Vancouver. Finally, on August 6, 1966, UFOs were seen in the sky of Esquimalt, on Vancouver Island. All the sightings occurred within a radius of 60 miles, in the most populated area of British Columbia, the Vancouver area and the east coast of the Vancouver Island.

Given the fragmented nature of the private observation system and the limited amount of data available for each case, it is quite difficult to push the analysis very far. At a more general level, however, a "coast-to-coast" symbolic signal seems visible, if one combines the data from both mini waves of the summer of 1966.

The Hamilton/Caledonia mini wave in 1967

The Hamilton/Caledonia area of Ontario, which is southwest

of Toronto, experienced a mini wave of its own in January and February 1967, with a short, but intense second outburst in June 1967. It included a prominent CE3 experience, and one of the rare Canadian "Men-in-Black" reports. The observations can be summed up as follows: night lights (NL) or daylight discs (DD) were observed over a two week period on January 29, and February 2, 6, 10, 11, and 14. The phenomenon showed more intensity on February 2; although it was only a night light, it moved in a zigzag way, with very high rates of speed, and displayed white and orange colors.

On February 14, a disc with red blinking lights was seen on a road and "forced" the driver of a car to go off road to avoid it. The object moved away in an open area and started to hover, and then landed on snowy field nearby. Landing marks were later found in the snow."[214]

The phenomenon then had a short, but intense outburst four months later on June 15, 1967. A close encounter of the third kind occurred near a factory by a Dofasco employee named Carmen Cuneo. He described seeing three objects near the ground for about 20 minutes; two were disc shaped; the other was cigar shaped and as big as a transport plane. He then saw three occupants, no more than four feet tall, in uniform and wearing helmets with four lights at each corner of its face. They were looking around the ground.[215] Some sources state that Cuneo then ran to get other people to look at what he saw, but upon arriving they only saw the objects moving away in the sky; no one could confirm seeing the occupants.[216] Another source states that when the others arrived even the objects were gone.[217] In any event, the objects left marks on the ground and, most importantly, an oily substance. The substance was brought in for analysis and was found to be ordinary lubricating oil.[218] As with many CE2 events, and as noted by Jacques Vallée on many occasions, the physical traces appear to be absurd. But, in fact, it might be the only valuable clue in this story.

Cuneo was apparently threatened by a Man-in-Black (MIB) and was told not to discuss his sighting further. The UFO DNA site states that he was physically visited on June 20, 1967, quoting the CUFOS database.[219] A MUFON bulletin of 1978 reported that Cuneo received a phone call from what he interpreted as an MIB on another day.[220] Some websites say the event occurred in 1976, leading one to wonder if it was a numeral inversion from 1967 to 1976, an error that was then reproduced by several other sites. In any case, the threats were just that, just as in other MIB reports.

As Peter Rojcewicz has observed, the MIB share the same narrative structure as meeting the Devil, where one is diverted from the truth in subtle ways.[221] In the case of the MIB, the threat that never materializes serves to reinforce the witnesses' belief that an "alien in spaceship" was involved, which pushes them even more to interpret and report the event as an ET encounter. This is congruent with an observation by parapsychologist Jule Eisenbud that the unconscious also creates a "defense mechanism" to protect its psi abilities by hiding them from ourselves.[222] In any event, this mini wave did not attract the attention of the authorities. The events were in all appearances localized and would have attracted only the interest of UFO organizations (the private observation system). This could be interpreted as an indication of intended audience that would be local.

Although this mini wave left very few clues, at least one symbolic trace is worth serious consideration: the oily substance. From a symbolic standpoint this is "pollution." The Hamilton area in the 1960s was indeed very polluted, particularly the air. For example, at the end of the two-month labor strike at the main steel mill in 1969, the air pollution levels were just starting to return to normal healthy levels.[223] This pollution issue was in fact so problematic, that the main industry in the area opened a research center dedicated to finding less polluting ways of producing steel.[224] Some of the key pollution from the production of steel is indeed oil coming from the coke burning.[225] The opening date of the research center was June 8, 1967, with many dignitaries present[226]—one week before the Cuneo's close encounter.

One would think that the opening of such a research center might have helped reduce local social tensions, therefore providing a less conducive social context for a psi-related event to occur. Yet the area in which the sightings occurred was a stronghold of the labor union movement (and still is to this day). It was also witnessing de-industrialization. During the 1950s, most of the textile mills closed. Then, in 1964 a major cigarette factory moved to a different region and a scale factory closed. In 1966, the Studebaker car factory plant closed as well. And early in the 1970s, a string of industrial closures occurred in the region. In fact, only the steel industry was still strong at the time.[227] In many ways, the industrial and economic prosperity of the region depended on the existence of this very polluting industry; it's something that people might have been aware of unconsciously but were not willing to talk about openly for fear of losing their jobs. This difficult situation can provide social tensions enabling psi effects to occur, and the limited clues available seem to point in that direction. In such a context, the opening of the center might have been seen as a ploy from the steel industry to put a band-aid on the problem while claiming publically they were doing something about it. In this light, these events could be interpreted as morphic resonance; in this case about pollution between different fields.

The Sudbury mini wave of 1967

The Sudbury area in northern Ontario also experienced a mini wave between September and November 1967, with an interesting sighting on October 4, the same day as the famous Shag Harbour incident, and another one on October 11, also the date of a second set of sightings near Shag Harbour.[228]

Most of the sightings are not spectacular in themselves, but in combination they create an interesting picture. Night lights and daylight discs were seen in the Sudbury area on August 29, observed by a Laurentian University professor; September 1, reported by amateur astronomers; and on September 9, 22, and 28. The October 4 sighting was described as very bright with red and green lights on of each side, with a pulsating white light in the middle. This might sound like an airplane, but it had no tail, and was said to be 200 feet long. The sighting lasted 2 hours, a very long time, and the object moved back and forth over the city while at a low altitude. These sightings were reported to the Canadian government's National Research Council.

Several independent witnesses observed a UFO on October 11. The Sudbury police received numerous reports, and at one point their radio system went down. One witness heard a loud noise from the sky but did not see anything. A local UFO organization received one report in October, but the date is unclear. It was reported that there was significant radio interference associated with the sighting of an object that produced a whining sound and almost landed in a field.[229]

On November 14 the Canadian Forces HQ asked for all the reports from the Sudbury police about these sightings. The military (hence the public observation system) was looking much more closely. As predicted by the MPI, this is also when a phenomenon starts to decline. There were only four more sightings of night-lights around Sudbury in 1967 after that.

October was the time when the phenomenon really "insisted" on being noted by the public authorities. Of note, at the time Sudbury was also going through major labor-related tensions during the 1960s.[230] But the date, in concordance with two well-noted events in Shag Harbour in Nova Scotia, points towards a more focused synchronicity.

There was one event that seemed very minor at the time, but it would have a very significant impact on Canadian national identity and social tensions in the years to come; it was the departure of René Lévesque from the Liberal Party of Quebec on October 14, 1967, three days after the last key sighting. He would go on to create the Movement Souveraineté-Association in November 1967, before merging his organization with another one to create the Parti Québécois in 1968, dedicated to making Quebec independent from Canada. In 1976, he and his party won the provincial election in Quebec and formed the provincial government. In 1980, he organized a referendum in Quebec to secede from Canada. He was defeated, but in 1995 his successors almost succeeded with 49.9% "yes" in favor of secession.

The 1960s were also quite significant for Canada in terms of collective identity. The country was finally coming of age symbolically, becoming separate from the British empire, by getting its own flag instead of the colonial one; its own National Anthem, replacing the British "God Save the Queen;" the federal government became officially bilingual French-English; and there was also the Universal Exhibition of 1967 (Expo 67) in Montreal, a major showcase for Canada at the time. The well-known Canadian journalist Pierre Berton wrote a book in the 1990s and, looking retrospectively, thought that 1967 was that last good year for Canada. The "party" for reaching adulthood was over for Canada after that. According to Berton, "in that sense, 1967 was the last good year before all Canadians began to be concerned about the future of our country."[231]

Furthermore, as noted by Berton, "The most significant event of 1967 was Charles de Gaulle's notorious 'Vive le Québec libre!' speech in Montreal in July. It gave the burgeoning separatist movement a new legitimacy, enhanced by René Lévesque's departure from the Liberal party later that year."[232]

Sudbury, also a bilingual English-French community, would have been seriously affected by a potential secession of Quebec from Canada. While Quebec is the heart of French-speaking Canada, the French-speaking communities outside Quebec would have been weakened by secession. The report provided by a local UFO organization about the loss of radio signals, combined with lots of white noise, could be symbolic of a community isolated from the rest of French-speaking Canada and submerged in lots of English "noise." The harmonious and more equalitarian relationships between the English and French communities of Canada were a major, if not the main, preoccupation of the federal government in the 1960s.

But could the synchronistic events of October 4 and 11 in Nova Scotia (Shag Harbour) be linked to unconscious worry on a national scale about the future of the country, and the core dynamics between the English and French-speaking Canadians? Interestingly, the Shag Harbour sightings were preceded by sightings over Quebec, as if it originated symbolically from there. There are some interesting synchronicities here, as well as possible morphic resonance between anxieties in the public mind and in the government about national identities.

The summer 1967 "visitations" cluster

Between the end of July and late August 1967, six close encounters of the third kind (CE3) were reported by the private UFO organizations. Given the rarity of CE3 in general, this concentration is unusual and can be seen as a form of "insistence" by the phenomenon to be "noted." The basic information on the sightings is as follow:

(1) At the end of July, in St-Stanislas-de-Kostka, Quebec, "11-year-old Denis Léger said a flying object, 'resembling a round and shiny saucer,' followed him for about 5 minutes, at 20-foot altitude, as he rode his bicycle. The bottom was made of glass 3 or 4 inches thick, and he could see three persons inside, one seated at one end and the others at the other end. 'They were small and black.'"[233]

(2) On August 12, in St-Louis-de-Kent, New Brunswick, a "dozen teens saw a 'huge, black monster' that descends from a lighted craft in the woods. The being was dressed in black, with a black face and goggles. They didn't approach, and it quickly disappeared."[234]

(3) On August 14, in St-Charles, New Brunswick, "an unidentified woman from St. Charles reported sighting a similar figure [similar to that of St-Louis-de-Kent] in the woods near the same road. The RCMP searched the area although they located a man dressed in black; there was no apparent connection with the encounters."[235]

(4) On August 15, in Port Perry, Ontario in "a farm area a young boy heard a loud oscillating sound, going over a nearby hill he saw a landed disc-shaped craft on four metallic legs, it was actually hovering just above the ground. On a platform around its perimeter, were seated eight to ten little men about three-foot tall, they wore tight fitting brown clothing. A depressed 12-foot

circular area was found on the ground later."[236]

(5) Also on August 15, in Welland, Ontario, a "family observed two bright lights traveling across the sky, through a pair of binoculars several figures could be seen moving in one of the lights. Both lights flew at high speed away from the area."[237]

(6) On August 23, in Joyceville, Ontario, while "driving from his home in Toronto early in the morning, Stanley Moxon saw a green light in a field off the road ahead of his car; he turned off his headlights and swung onto a side road to get closer. Turning his lights on again, he saw a huge craft shaped like two saucers put together, and two human like entities about four-feet high in white uniforms and helmets. They 'seemed to be at work around the machine;' when they were discovered, they quickly jumped into the object, which took off silently at tremendous speed."[238]

Taken together, these reports seem unrelated and unexplainable. As there is only scant information about each of them, it is difficult to make a detailed analysis. Yet if one looks beyond the surface, there are a number of commonalities. All the reporting was local only. In cases 1, 2, 4, and 5, children were involved, and given the inherent bias against younger witnesses, these cases were not likely to reach the public authorities. Cases 3 and 6 were reported by adults who sought out the local police (note that the RCMP plays the role of the local police in rural areas of New Brunswick, as part of an agreement between the province and the federal government). Yet the police did not report these events further to the federal government, either the military or the National Research Council. This is an important clue—the phenomenon did not appear to seek the attention of the larger society. Besides, knowledge of the CE3 cluster was not possible at that time; one case surfaced in 1968 and two others surfaced only in 1979.

It is therefore possible to think that separate local psi effects could be held responsible for those events. From a symbolic perspective, let's note the importance of the "children" involved in these sightings, not only the witnesses, but in three cases the entities were perceived as being of child-size (1, 4, and 6). In most cases, the entities did not engage with the witnesses but were either scared or oblivious to presence of witnesses (child-like behavior?). Could the symbolic message be about refusing to grow-up, as Pierre Berton noted about the Canadian mood in 1967?

The 1967 national tensions cluster

The three most noted cases from the Canadian UFO wave of 1966-67 occurred in 1967. They are, in chronological order, the Falcon Lake incident of May 20, the Duhamel crop circles of August 8, and the Shag Harbour "crash" of October 4. When the Department of National Defence (DND) transferred its files to the National Research Council (NRC), these three cases were specifically highlighted in a November 1967 letter as meriting particular attention. DND wanted to be kept abreast of any findings by the NRC.[239] Clearly, in those cases the phenomenon was able to get the attention of the public authorities. Once again, we have three cases that on the surface seem to be unrelated. When taken in isolation and separately, they seem profoundly absurd and meaningless. Although these cases were better investigated than most of the other cases of 1966-67 because the public authorities had stepped in, nothing worth of mentioning emerged from their analysis. But by integrating a social psi perspective in light of morphic resonance, a different image emerges that is actually quite consistent with the other clusters where public authorities got involved: Canadian national tensions are symbolically found across all these cases.

Falcon Lake incident

The details of this incident are available through many sources. This is the synopsis of the case prepared by DND in its letter to the NRC:

"A Mr. Steven Michalak of Winnipeg, Manitoba reported that he had come into physical contact with a UFO during a prospecting trip in the Falcon Lake area, some 90 miles east of

Winnipeg on the 20 May 1967. Mr. Michalak stated that he was examining a rock formation when two UFOs appeared before him. One of the UFOs remained airborne in the immediate area for a few moments, then flew off at great speed. The second UFO landed a few hundred feet away from his position. As he approached the UFO, a side door opened and voices were heard from within. Mr. Michalak stated that he approached the object, but was unable to see due to a bright yellow bluish light which blocked his vision. He endeavoured to communicate with the personnel inside the object, but without result. As he approached within a few feet of the object, the door closed, he heard a whining noise and the object commenced to rotate anti-clockwise and finally raised off the ground. He reached out with his left gloved hand and touched the object prior to its lifting off the ground; the glove burned immediately as he touched the object. As the object left the ground, the exhaust gases burned his cap, out and inner garments and he sustained rather severe stomach and chest burns. As a result of this he was hospitalized for a number of days. The doctors who interviewed and attended Mr. Michalak were unable to obtain any information that could account for the burns to his body. The personal items of clothing which were alleged to have been burned by the UFO were subjected to an extensive analysis at the SCNF Crime Laboratory. The analysis was not able to reach any conclusion as to what may have caused the burn damage. Soil samples taken from the immediate area occupied by the UFO by Mr. Michalak were analyzed and found to be radioactive to a degree that the samples had to be safely disposed of. An examination of the alleged UFO landing area was tested by a radiologist from the Department of Health and Welfare and a small area was found radioactive. The radiologist was unable to provide an explanation as to what caused this area to become contaminated. Both DND and RCMP investigation teams were unable to provide evidence which would dispute Mr. Michalak's story."[240]

A few more elements emerged from other sources. A 1968 analysis and a 1979 re-evaluation showed that the radioactive contamination was likely from natural uranium ore and associated radon gas emanations.[241]

From a symbolic perspective this event has several clues to offer. First of all, the location is an interesting one. Falcon Lake was named after Pierre Falcon, a French-speaking poet of Métis origin who lived in the 19th century (1793-1876). The Métis were made up of people having both European (mostly French) and Native American ancestry. They lived in Western Canada, mostly in Manitoba, Saskatchewan, and Alberta. Their history is a sad one, as they were victims of the racist attitudes of the British authorities, and many had their land confiscated and given to British settlers. They defended themselves on several occasions but were defeated by the British Army and the white settlers. Their French-speaking heritage also disappeared over time; they became almost fully anglicized. Pierre Falcon actually wrote songs and poems describing the fight against the English-speaking settlers and the injustice the Métis people were facing.[242]

There are other symbolic clues in the events. Michalak meet "people" speaking a language he did not understand. He was burnt in the forest, which is actually how Pierre Falcon described his compatriots the "Bois-Brûlé," or "burnt wood."[243] Radioactivity was not known in the 19th century, so this clue might be a bit subtler. In the 1960s, there was no uranium mining in Manitoba. The closest such mines were in Northern Saskatchewan, and in Ontario in Elliot Lake, all far from Flacon Lake.[244] Elliott Lake was a key uranium-mining town then and was also a mixed French-English community. Finally, it is worth noting that on the day before the incident, on May 19, 1967, the Premier of Quebec, Daniel Johnson, came back from an official visit from France, where he was received as a Head of State, a prelude to the famous "Vive le Québec libre!" of De Gaulle a few weeks later.

Duhamel crop circles

In 1967, the expression "crop circles" did not exist, but the association between UFOs and what we call today crop circles is not a new one. In the 1950s they were known as "saucer nests" by some American UFO organizations. But it was something new for Canada in the 1960s. The "crop circles" were thought to be connected to UFOs, because "For several weeks before the crop circles appeared, Duhamel had been plagued with strange occurrences. Reports of unidentified flying objects had made it into the local papers weeks before the crop circles were discovered."[245] The official synopsis described the events:

"On August 8 1967, a Mr. K. Patrige, of Camrose, Alberta, reported the finding of a number of circular impressions in a pasture in the vicinity of the town of Camrose, Alberta. An investigation was conducted by an officer from Canadian Forces Base, Edmonton, in the company of Dr. G. H. Jones, of the Defence Research Board Experimental Station in Suffield.

"All the marks exhibited the same general appearance; a ring six inches in width, with diameter varying from slightly over 31 feet to 36 feet. No evidence of heat was evident, but a definite impression in the ground, which was soft from recent rains, indicated distinct pressure. Some slight evidence of movement in a radial manner along the marks was visible in that the grass had been pressed down in a definite direction.

"No evidence that would lead to the conclusion of deliberate interference or involvement of any person was found, nor was there any trace of chemical or radioactivity in the area."[246]

This noted UFO incident is also linked symbolically to the Métis. The area was a Métis settlement in the 19th century, originally called "La Boucane," named after the first Métis settlers, and renamed after the French-Canadian Roman Catholic Bishop of Ottawa Mgr. Duhamel.[247] Like a crop circle, they left their mark, but soon it would disappear both physically and from memory.

A key document, which emerged recently, was a draft letter signed on August 2, 1967, by René Lévesque announcing his resignation from the Liberal Party of Quebec to the then leader of the Party. The actual resignation took place on October 14, 1967, and set in motion a series of major events in Canada, as discussed previously. A paragraph in this letter is highly symbolic and could have been applied very well to the Métis of Duhamel:

"C'est bien ainsi que l'ont compris tous ceux qui ne nous aiment pas. Il y en a un grand nombre au Canada, même parmi nous, de ces gens qui endurent les Canadiens français à condition qu'ils soient bien sages, qu'ils ne se prennent pas pour "d'autres" et qu'ils confirment périodiquement l'image rassurante qu'on s'acharne à se faire d'eux: la pittoresque survivance indigène appelée tôt ou tard à se perdre gentiment dans le paysage."[248]

[It is in this way that those who do not like us have understood it. There are many people in Canada, even among us, who tolerate the French-Canadians only on the condition that they be quiet, that they do not think of themselves as important, and that they confirm periodically the reassuring picture painted of them: this picturesque survival of indigenous people which would, sooner or later, gently disappear from the scenery.]

The Shag Harbour "crash"

The Shag Harbour case is arguably the best-known UFO case from Canada, and maybe for this reason some people have dubbed it the "Canadian Roswell."[249] It was also one of the cases evaluated by the Condon committee. Here is the official description of the events:

"An RCMP corporal and six other witnesses observed what they believed to be an unidentified flying object off the south-west coast of Nova Scotia, Canada on the 4th October 1967. The object was described as approximately 60 feet in length and was flying in an easterly direction when first sighted. During their observation, the UFO descended rapidly to the surface and made a 'bright splash' as it struck the water. For some time after the impact, a single white light remained on the surface. The RCMP corporal endeavoured to reach the floating white object, but unfortunately, before he could reach the location the object sank. A search of the area failed to produce any material evidence, which could assist in explaining or establishing the identity of the object. An underwater search conducted by divers from the Department of National Defence also failed to locate any tangible evidence, which could be used to arrive at an explainable conclusion."[250]

Furthermore, the government examination of the case produced some more interesting evidence. On the evening of October 4, 1967, the pilots of an Air Canada jetliner flying over Saint-Jean in Quebec, southeast of Montreal, witnessed the following, as reported later to the authorities: "Flying on top of layered clouds, well below us. The Captain drew my attention to an unusual set of lights to the south. One large bright white light and six small ones. It looks like a large kite about 20 deg. above the horizon at 90 degs from the aircraft. While we were looking at this set of lights we saw a big fire ball that started as a very bright white light and grew into a large red ball. It then turns violet in color, then light blue. We saw two of these. I checked the clock. The first one was at 19:19 EDT the second at 19:31 EDT. At 19:35 EDT one large pear shape cloud glowing pale blue was drifting slowly eastward."[251]

Private researchers were also able to get the some additional details.[252] According to Ledger and Styles, several witnesses in the area around Halifax saw strange lights moving towards the southwest along the coast, between 21:00 ADT until 23:00 ADT. The observations then moved to Lunenburg, and then Waymouth, to finally around Shag Harbor for the last observations.[253] Several witnesses on Cape Sable Island described the descent into water of the objects as a "falling-leaf motion."[254]

This last observation is particularly interesting as it is a motion noted in a number of poltergeist events. But not only did the overall event start in Quebec, the French-speaking province of Canada, ten days before René Lévesque's critical political move, it occurred in another area of past French-English tensions. Cape Sable Island was also the point of departure of several deportation ships, bringing in harsh conditions, and taking the French-speaking Acadiens away from their land so that English settlers could have it.

Symbolically, we have something emanating from Quebec and showing the color blue in the sky, blue being the color associated with the movement seeking the independence of Quebec, that sinks into the sea in a place where British cruelty towards the French-Canadians took place, sending people to their death at sea. The fact that an agent of the state witnessed it is also indicative that the phenomenon might have been seeking the attention of the public authorities. If this was not enough to get the government's attention, it also "crashed" near one of the nodes of a top secret underwater submarine detection network, put in place in the context of the Cold War against Soviet submarine intrusion. In a way, the phenomenon "took no chances"—it wanted to be noticed by the authorities, and as in any macro psi event, when observation becomes too intense, the phenomenon loses its indeterminacy and stops. The Shag Harbour incident marks the decline phase of the 1966-67 Canadian UFO wave. And as in most RSPK or poltergeist events, those for whom the message was intended did not understand it. A similar symbolic message was resonating across different time fields, physical fields, and collective mental fields about Canadian identities and tensions.

The analysis of the Canadian 1966-1967 UFO wave is instructive in a number of ways. There is a striking concordance between geographic locations, dates of UFO events, and dates of significant social events with the key symbolism. These cases, when linked together within a proper analytical framework, start to make sense. It would be interesting to do a similar analysis of the American UFO wave of 1966-67 and find links to it in the racial riots and social tensions experienced in 1966 and especially in 1967.

The events that were noted by the private UFO organizations are much more difficult to interpret, in large part because they were not approached from the "broader" perspective, leaving very little data to work with. Some cases were investigated in some depth, but with the passing of time, such information can become extremely difficult to find. In some cases, like the APRO reports on the case, the evidence is locked up in private hands not willing to share it. Furthermore, if these sightings were intended to be observed by other than the public authorities, then the message should logically be intended for a local or private audience, making the investigation that much harder as one would need to get detailed knowledge of unconsciously perceived local issues.

It is important to emphasize that a deeper understanding of many sightings of the 1966-67 wave are beyond our reach simply because they were likely meant to be meaningful only to the witnesses themselves. Some other sightings are likely to be misperceptions and hoaxes, but these others sightings, including the hoaxes, could be seen as synchronistic events that participated in creating a social psi event by keeping the attention on the phenomenon. The theory of morphic resonance is about information propagating into different fields. But how it propagates or resonates can be through various simultaneous forms, whether through normal means, synchronicity, psi, social psi or hoaxing. At very least, this case encourages us to maintain a wide-open view when dealing with diffused UFO events.

Chapter 8
The Barney and Betty Hill Story Revisited

During the night of September 19, 1961, Barney and Betty Hill were driving back home through a lonely road in central New Hampshire. They were returning from a short vacation in Canada, on their way back to Portsmouth. They saw a strange light in the night sky, and they thought at first that it was a plane. But the light seemed to follow them and gradually got closer. They eventually stopped the car to get a better view of the light with binoculars. Barney saw a bright object near the ground and strange people around it. He panicked and drove away in a hurry.

What happened afterward was a mystery to the Hill couple. They came to realize that while they were just 35 miles away from where they had stopped, in an area known as Indian Head, two hours had elapsed. But they could not remember what happened during those two hours. Barney started to have strange dreams and was obviously stressed. Betty, too, had strange dreams. They eventually decided to see a mental health specialist. With therapist Dr. Benjamin Simon, they underwent hypnotic regression. While in trance, they both described being abducted by alien beings and brought in a spacecraft to undergo some sort of strange medical examination.

Before going to see the Dr. Simon, the Hill couple met UFO investigators to tell them about their experience, and they related to them a number of unusual events. Their watches had stopped working on the night of their UFO incident, Barney's shoes were seriously damaged, Betty's dress was damaged and dirty in a few places, and there were shinny spots on the car trunk that appeared to be magnetized. The Hills' story was eventually written up in *The Interrupted Journey* by John Fuller in 1966, and made into a TV movie, *The UFO Incident*, in 1975. The Hill story became the prototype of the many UFO abduction stories that emerged during the next three decades.

There is little doubt that both Barney and Betty were sincere in recounting their conscious experience, and a very competent medical doctor had hypnotized them.

For many in the UFO community, the Hill story constitutes strong evidence to support their belief in the extraterrestrial hypothesis. For others, it was just a regular UFO sighting that became embellished throughout the years, and the story that emerged under hypnotic regression was just dreams mixed up with fantasies. What can we make of this story? Was it really an alien encounter or just a fantasy?

This is a standard synopsis of the Barney and Betty Hill story. But like most well publicized UFO events, the Hills' story has often been presented in ways that reinforce the belief that UFOs are spacecraft piloted by alien beings. Some of the basic facts are not always presented, while others are presented in a non-critical way. The Hill story is actually more complex than it appears, and like many UFO encounters contains elements that do not make much sense. But when viewed from a parapsychological perspective, the Hill story can make better sense.

A different approach to a well-known story
The first thing to keep in mind is that at the conscious level, namely in their pre-hypnotized account of the events, the Hill couple did not clearly see a craft. Both Barney and Betty saw something with naked eyes and with binoculars while they were conscious, and it was described as something that "appeared to be flashing thin pencils of different colored lights, rotating around an object which at that time appeared cigar shaped. Just a moment before it had changed its speed from slow to fast, and then slowed down again as it crossed the face of the moon. The lights were flashing persistently, red amber, green and blue."[255] This description does not provide a lot of information, and is rather unclear if the UFO was a manufactured craft. Also, it is important to note that at the end of the event, as told under regression, the "spaceship" was actually perceived as an orange ball of fire,[256] which is typical of the most common form of earthlights.

Some well-known pro-ETH ufologists have claimed that the UFO was tracked on radar during the night of September 19 to

20, 1961, over central New Hampshire, thereby proving the Hills' story. But after the research by David Webb and John Oswald in the 1970s, it became clear that there is no evidence of a link between the radar tracking and the Hill incident.[257]

There are other physical elements, all equivocal, that are cited as proof of the reality of the Hill encounter being an ET event. One concerns the marks found on the top of Barney's shoes. It should be remembered that the Hills stopped in a forested area. Walking through the brush at night could easily have produced such marks on his shoes. Likewise for the broken zipper and marks on Betty's dress; it too could have been damaged while walking in the forest, perhaps by getting stuck on a branch, and the marks themselves could have been caused by tree resin; these marks were found to be of Earthly biological origin.[258] These two items point towards the Hills taking a walk— which they did not remember taking—in the forest during their return trip to Portsmouth.

More problematic are the magnetized marks that appeared on the car. But if the orange ball of fire they reported under hypnosis was actually an earthlight, and since smaller balls of light are known to accompany larger ones, as noted with the Hessdalen earthlights,[259] then perhaps the "perfectly" round and magnetized marks noted by Barney and Betty on their car could be explained by the impact of such smaller balls of light. In any event, those mark do not constitute a proof of any ET involvement.

Most of the information about the Hills' close encounter essentially comes from the accounts of Betty and Barney's recollection of events while in altered states of consciousness during the hypnotic regression sessions with Dr. Simon. With this kind of evidence, a simple materialistic explanation, as proposed by the proponents of the ETH, is difficult to maintain. There are good reasons to think, like Dr. Simon, that something happened to them while they were in an altered state of consciousness in the forest of New Hampshire, but the physical evidence put forward does not really allow for a sound analysis.

A closer look at psychokinesis in UFO events

The Hills' story is relatively well documented when it comes to their testimony both in a conscious and hypnotic state. It was also a well-circumscribed event. But given it was also a one-time event, the four phase model of the MPI is less applicable to their story. But the notion of morphic resonance is useful in putting the specific events in a larger context. What is missing in most reports of the case is an approach that looks at the Hills' story at the more local and personal level. While the notion of morphic resonance can help explain the impersonal aspects of the event, something else is needed to make sense of the personal dimensions.

One of the very few approaches that might provide new insights on the Hills' story is one proposed by those who study psychokinetic events in general, not just RSPK. Pamela Heath, a parapsychologist whose interest is psychokinesis, wrote a substantial work entitled *The PK Zone* (2003). Based on her research, it turns out that a number of PK features present striking similarities to the events told by Betty and Barney Hill.

One of the key conclusions in Heath's research is that an altered state of consciousness (ASC) is a pervasive element in PK events. Heath found that PK is more likely to occur when there is:

(1) a feeling of being in another dimension or alternate reality;

(2) an awareness of discarnate entities, by accessing our spirit;

(3) an altered sense of time or of being "out" of the time;

(4) a sense of vast complexity, difficult for the ordinary mind to understand;

(5) a sense of flow, or being in the "zone;"

(6) a fusion between the conscious and the unconscious;

(7) a sense of meditation; and

(8) a subtle shift in the quality of the experience.[260]

These elements, of course, cover a wide variety of PK experiences from lab tests involving random number generators to poltergeist events. Elements (1) to (3) in particular, describe very well many UFO close encounters. It's what UFO researcher Jenny Randles calls the "Oz factor,"[261] where UFO witnesses of close encounters of the third kind are often in a trance or dream-like state. Randles explains: "the Oz factor certainly points to consciousness as the focal point of the UFO encounter... Subjective data that override objective reality could be internal [from our subconscious], external [e.g., from some other intelligent agency], or both...The encounter has a visionary component. You might interpret that as meaning it is all in the imagination. But it really means that there is a direct feed, if you like, from the source of the encounter to the consciousness of the witness...Some witnesses report a strange sensation prior to the encounter—a sort of mental tingling as if they are aware that something is about to happen. They just have to look up and see what is there, as if it had called to them silently...Then time seems to disappear and lose all meaning."[262]

The Hills' experience definitely displays the Oz Factor. Under hypnosis during the February 22, 1964, session, Barney described that he saw the Cheshire cat in Alice in Wonderland disappear, that the eyes on the face of the "leader" were disconnected from his body, and that the leader's was "just floating about."[263] Both Betty and Barney encountered strange entities that could access their mind directly; this is very similar to an awareness of discarnate entities. And it is well known that the Hills were missing for a few hours, which they could not account for. They both experienced a sense of altered time. The same occurred under hypnosis. During the March 7, 1964, session, Betty said "We're driving along ... I don't know where we are ... I don't even know how we got here ... Barney and I, we were driving, I don't know how long...I don't know how long..."[264]

Heath found that among those who report PK experiences there is a general sense of knowing among experiencers,[265] knowing that the event will occur, for example. On numerous occasions, Barney and Betty stated that they knew that the light in the sky was "interested" in them. For instance, Barney said during the session on February 22, 1964, that "the object was still around us. I could feel it around us. I saw it when we passed by the object. When I got in the car, it had swung around so that it was out there. I—I know it was out there."[266] They also reported knowing what the alien entities were saying even when no sounds or spoken words were uttered.

ILLUMINATIONS

Other factors that are more commonly found in spontaneous PK are strong emotions and a strong sense of playfulness. Heath noted that "peak levels of emotion can trigger PK, especially for spontaneous events. This seemed to be true for a wide variety of strong emotions, including anger, frustration with others, sadness, excitement, and love."[267] To illustrate the role of playfulness, Heath quotes an experiencer as saying: "play is very important in these sorts of things...its entertainment at a certain level...it has a thrilling quality."[268] Emotions tend to run high in UFO experiences as well; often fear is mixed with curiosity. Both Barney and Betty showed a high degree of fear about the aliens and the craft during the hypnosis sessions.

But there was also a playful aspect. For instance, Betty said during the session of March 21, 1964: "I was more curious and interested. And I had the feeling of being sort of helpless. That something was going to happen, and I didn't have much control over it. But I wasn't really afraid. I guess I was looking forward to it."[269] During the March 28, 1964, session Barney said that he was fascinated while at the same time afraid.[270] It is also interesting to note Barney said that the fascination "was being produced by something stronger than me, outside me, that I wasn't creating this."[271] Heath found that PK was also associated with what she calls a sense of energy, which may be felt as if it is coming from a "higher source."[272]

Heath describes openness as "both something of a personality style and a lack of rigid beliefs that might prohibit PK. It seems to indicate a flexible worldview, which might allow the performer not only to do PK, but to also recognize and accept their experiences. [But...] belief systems seemed to play far less of a role than the literature would suggest."[273] This finding was corroborated in other studies[274] that identified the belief in the paranormal as an important element of the UFO experience. They used the concept of belief to mean a positive attitude towards the paranormal in general.

In her summary, Heath reassesses her findings, stating that "in a way, openness to an experience is also a willingness to suspend disbelief, and to see what can happen without the interference of the intellect. It also suggests a lack of attachment to a rigid world view. Hence, it is possible that beliefs could act to modify PK performance either through encouraging the performer to be open to the possibility of PK, and/or willingness to open up to that state...."[275]

Although Betty appears to have had no conscious interest in UFOs prior to her September 1961 experience, it is clear from the onset that she thought the light in the sky was an alien spaceship. She immediately linked that experience with one her sister Janet had related; she had seen a UFO during the 1950s. Indeed, Betty called Janet not long after she arrived home to discuss her UFO experience. Another fact rarely underlined by ufologists is that Betty engaged in informal telepathic experiments with Barney before their UFO event,[276] and that her family had a history of paranormal encounters.[277] Lastly, she claimed to have had other UFO sightings in 1966-67.[278]

Barney, on the other hand, was clearly struggling not to believe it was an "alien spaceship." This struggle was obvious while he was under hypnosis with Dr. Simon.[279] Such a conflict was clearly indicative that while he unconsciously accepted the possibility of an "alien spaceships," he was consciously trying to resist such "irrational belief." In the end, they had a different experience. Barney had a more rigid belief in "rationality," while Betty was quite open to have an extraordinary experience. Barney had no visual memories of being on "the ship." It was Betty who provided the bulk of the story about the "greys," the medical experiment, the stellar map, etc. Hence, the Hills' story also fits well with Heath's findings on openness. Although it is not possible to prove without a doubt that the Hills' story was actually a spontaneous PK experience, it is clear their story has a lot in common with what is known about the psychosocial dynamics of PK.

The physical evidence points towards the Hills stopping on the side of the road and walking in an altered state of consciousness in a wooded area. What emerged from the hypnotic regression is a description that matches quite well the psychological state of mind of someone having a PK experience. In other words, they seemed to be in a situation that enhances the probability of substantive spontaneous psi effects.

A more complex event than it appears

One of the key conclusions put forward by Dr. Simon in June 1964 was that the part of the Hills' story onboard the "spaceship" was most likely a fantasy born out of Betty's dream and absorbed through a kind of osmosis by Barney.[280] A number of elements could be presented to support this thesis. Betty had her dreams a few weeks after the events in the fall of 1961 and wrote them down. The Hills consulted for the first time with Dr. Simon in December 1963. So that's a span of two years between these events, which is a lot of time for elaboration, contamination, and discussion with her husband. ETH proponents claimed that the Hill couple never discussed their dreams, and that Barney never read her written account of them. This is, in fact, incorrect. Many details were discussed between them.[281] Betty also recounted publicly the content of her dreams before 1964 during a meeting where Barney was in the attendance.

There was also an active nurturing of the phenomenon. Regardless of what happened in September 1961, it is clear that the Hill couple was engaged in a psychosocial dynamic that reinforced the ETH interpretation of their experience. It is important to note that after the events, Barney was not sure what to make of what had happened to them, while Betty made the UFO-alien connection immediately. In a process similar to Marian apparitions where a beautiful lady becomes the Virgin Mary when religious people get involved, the ETH community quickly welcomed the Hills, and the Hills in turn absorbed the belief system of that community. Their interactions with ufologists in the weeks following their incident at Indian Head could not have been without an impact.

As noted previously, the first call Betty made was to her sister who saw a UFO, and her sister provided Betty with information as to how to report their sighting.[282] Betty told the story to their tenants the same day,[283] and then some of her friends and co-workers later on.[284] Betty also called the local Air Force base to report her sighting.[285] Finally, Betty borrowed Major Keyhoe's famous book on UFOs, a pro-ETH work, at the local library, read it in one sitting, and wrote to Keyhoe's National Investigations of Committee on Aerial Phenomena (NICAP) on September 26, 1961, to report the sighting.[286] All of these actions were taken while Barney expressed his reluctance at every turn.

On October 21, 1961, the Hills agreed to meet NICAP investigator Walter Webb.[287] After a discussion with Major Keyhoe about the Hill case, Robert Hohman and C.D Jackson decided to interview the Hills as well; this occurred on November 25, 1961. A friend of the Hills, Major MacDonald, joined them as well. It's important to note that it was only at this point that they realized there was a missing time period for which they could not account during the early hours of September 20, 1961.[288] In other words, the missing time only emerged as part of the investigation by ufologists. Later on, the Hills presented their story at a few UFO-related public meetings. And before long, what was a very odd and bizarre encounter came to be viewed as the prime example of an extraterrestrial visitation.

On March 25, 1962, as Barney's physical and mental health was deteriorating, the Hills met Dr. Quirke for an interview; he suggested a cooling off period in the hopes that things would get back to normal.[289] Yet the Hills pursued the issue, even making frequent trips to Indian Head where they thought the event had taken place.[290]

By the time the Hills came to see Dr. Simon, a lot of UFO information was already part of their conscious mind. For instance, during the session of March 7, 1964, Betty said that "… I kept wondering why they were following us. And as I would figure that, I was wondering if they were as curious about me as I was about them." When Dr. Simon asked, "you speak of 'they'?" Betty replied, "I mean, well, I figured there must be somebody inside of the object, you know, someone directing its flight. And so, whoever was inside, this is 'they.'"[291] Given the unfolding of events between September 1961 and March 1964, such a statement from Betty could be seen as equivocal. Either she was not truthful when she said she had no particular preconceptions about UFOs, or her statement under hypnosis is the product of a psychosocial process that occurred after the actual events took place.

For Barney, on the other hand, there was an additional dynamic at play. The UFO incident clearly illustrated that Barney was the one who was most challenged by all of this, especially about his identity as an African-American man married to a white woman in the 1960s. The hypnotic regression showed that issue was a constant preoccupation for him. For instance, when they were driving through Montreal in the afternoon prior to the event, he was worried about how the French-Canadians would react towards him and was relieved to see other blacks walking in the city streets.[292] He had the same apprehension in the restaurant where they stopped before crossing the border.[293] When he was looking into the binoculars towards the "spaceship," his first reaction was that he saw an "Irishman friendly to Blacks," which was described as a rare thing by Barney.[294] Then the image changed and he saw a Nazi officer, which upset him greatly.[295] Even if it was clear to Dr. Simon that the couple displayed no particular signs of tensions given their different backgrounds,[296] being black in white person's world clearly affected Barney, a quite common feeling in the 1960s, as the studies conducted by psychiatrist Frantz Fanon showed.[297]

The Hills' story is complex. On one hand, their experience seems concordant with what is known about the paranormal dimension of the UFO enigma. On the other hand, there is also plenty of evidence that between the incident of September 1961 and the first hypnotic regression with Dr. Simon a few years later, the Hills had a lot of opportunities to create a make-believe story. Like in most paranormal stories, their personal story seems to be a mixed bag. The next issue is assessing whether there were impersonal elements involved, also of a paranormal nature.

The Hills' experience and morphic fields

In the third week of September 1961, there was a lot of going on in the United States that related to the Hills' story. At least two major releases of emotional energy occurred around this date.

As Martin Kottmeyer and Pierre Viéroudy have noted,[298]

important UFOlogical events in the United States appear to be linked to national security concerns. In September 1961, the world was in the midst of the Berlin crisis, which brought about a very serious confrontation between the United States and the Soviet Union. On September 21, 1961, the day after the Hill event, a secret National Intelligence Estimate (NIE) was circulated among senior decision makers showing that the Soviet Union was bluffing—they could not back up their claim to West Berlin with a large force of nuclear missiles.[299] To the great relief of President Kennedy, preparations for an eventual pre-emptive nuclear strike were no longer necessary. This also indicated that America was no longer in catch-up mode, which had been the perception since the launch of Sputnik in 1957; in fact, America was clearly ahead in the Cold War contest. There was no "missile gap."

Second, the Civil Rights movement was actively engaged in "Freedom Rides" during the summer and fall of 1961. These Freedom Rides had roots in the famous Rosa Parks incident of 1955, where both white and black activists rode coach buses across the southern United States, purposefully transgressing segregation laws in bus seating arrangements. This led to several violent incidents where racist demonstrators burned buses. Many Civil Rights activists were seriously beaten and arrested by the police in states where segregation was enforced. On September 22, 1961, two days after the Hills' incident, the Freedom Rides Civil Rights activists won their first victory with a ruling from the Federal Interstate Commerce Commission prohibiting segregation in trains, buses, and transportation terminals across the country.[300] Given the Hills' active involvement in the National Association for the Advancement of Colored People (NAACP), these "interrupted journeys" at the border of segregationist states in the south were certainly known to them.

What is important to realize is that these key events occurred one and two days *after* the Hills' UFO encounter. This could be seen as a form of precognition linked to America's self-identity both as a superpower and as society filled with racial tensions. On one hand America was no longer the underdog in the Cold

War competition, and the Civil Rights activists were becoming successful in changing American society. To use Benedict Anderson's analysis of national myths,[301] it is clear that deeply shared myths and their unconscious underpinnings about America's identity were seriously affected at that time. The key issue, then, is to determine if there was morphic resonance across fields that would have shaped in an impersonal way the Hills' UFO experience.

Elements of morphic resonance
The first interesting link that can be made involves the Hills' description of the "alien spacecraft" and the coach buses used by the Freedom Riders. Was what the Hills saw a mixture of flying saucer and coach bus, a kind of flying bus? Here is the famous drawing made by Barney Hill:

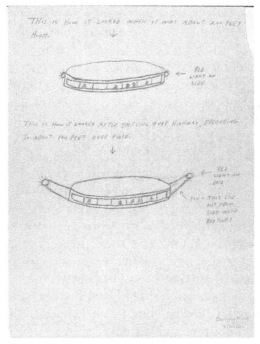

Drawing made by Barney Hill of what he saw during his UFO experience[302]

It is interesting to note that they also described red lights at each end of the object. As it happens, the coach buses contemporary to the Hill event had red lights on top at each end:

Typical coach bus of the early 1960s[303]

Another symbolic match concerns the appearance of the "grey aliens" that could have caused Barney's panic as he looked through the binoculars. If one looks at the "classic" grey representation upside down and compare with a hood of the infamous racist organization Klu Klux Klan, a striking similarity emerges, as shown here:

Member of the racist organization Klu Klux Klan in ceremonial dress[304]

Inverted mask of a Grey alien as usually portrayed in popular culture[305]

During the hypnotic regression, the issue of sexual reproduction clearly took center stage. Barney's semen was collected, and Betty's pregnancy test through the navel used a technology that was just about to be discovered, but that is now regarded as low tech by present-day standards.[306] There is also the issue of the skin test performed on Betty;[307] let's remember that grey is a color produced out of a mixture of black and white. And their captors are creatures now known as "the Greys."

Although a medical condition prevented Betty from having children,[308] the subject of mixed-race children in the United States of the 1960s was not to be taken lightly. The issue of interracial marriages was not just a contested social convention in the United States at the time. It was against the law in many states; these laws were in place to avoid mixed offspring known in the racist literature as miscegenation. Not until 1967, with the landmark decision of the U.S. Supreme Court in the case of *Loving vs. Virginia*, were the laws prohibiting interracial marriages formally declared unconstitutional. But not until 2000 did the last state, Alabama, formally strike down its anti-interracial marriage law (though it had not been enforced).[309]

The last symbolic element addressed here is the famous star map that was first described by Betty in terms of 1960s paper technology, i.e. a regular map.[310] But was much later "re-assessed" by Betty as being a digital display while she went under hypnosis under the guidance of her niece (an ETH ufologist), at a time when such technology was widely available on Earth.[311] An astronomer later analyzed the star map by computer. Given the relative position of the stars on Betty's recollection of the map, the astronomer concluded that it was a representation of the Zeta Reticuli star system. There are a number of problems with the Zeta Reticuli hypothesis, however. Since it is based on memory, Betty's drawing of the map can only be considered approximate. There are also an almost infinite number of possibilities if one expands the possible stars beyond 100 light years, etc.

If one reverses the "stellar" map and compares it with a map showing the Freedom Ride action of 1961, but not published until 1962, the similarities are quite interesting.

Inverted starmap produced from Betty Hill's original hand drawn map seen during her UFO experience[312]

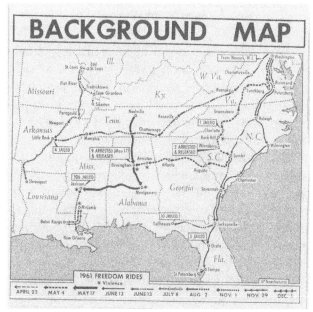

Newspaper clipping of 1962 showing the route taken by the Freedom Riders[313]

When taken together, these symbolic elements can be interpreted as social psi propagating through morphic resonance. It also suggests that whatever happened to the Hills had a significant paranormal component. But it is also possible that some elements of their descriptions were indeed unconscious reconstruction of events after the fact, and that the wider social events of the early 1960s fed the "fantasy" that Dr. Simon was talking about.

In the Hill case, various symbolic elements could be seen as resonating in the social realm, in the minds of the Hills, and possibly in physical reality itself. The conjunction of dates with two major social events (the Berlin crisis and the Freedom ride first victory), the symbolic view of the "ship" as a bus, the "alien" appearance, the "alien" behavior in the light of the racial tensions of 1961, the direct involvement of the witnesses with the Civil Rights movement, and Barney's internal psychological tensions about these social issues, all provide a case for an event with a social psi component, even if other elements may not be psi-related.

The most interesting aspect of the Hill story, however, is that it went on to repeat itself numerous times, what became known close encounters of the fourth kind (alien abductions) or CE4. No unequivocal physical trace has ever been produced in the many CE4s documented since the 1960s. Many of those experiences also appear to be a mixture of things, ranging from down-to-earth traumatic events unconsciously disguised as a UFO encounter to pure make-believe reinforced by unscrupulous ufologists, as well as some possibly strange experiences. It seems that although the Hills' story was shaped in the backdrop of racial tensions and a changing society, somehow the construct of the experience crystallized into this "grey" abduction storyline that apparently resonated in the mental field of many others who had no particular challenges about racial identity. In a way, it seems that a very personal set of information about racial tensions for the Hills became an impersonal force affecting others through morphic resonance.

Chapter 9
The Political Sociology of Alien Encounters

The UFO phenomenon has been associated with the visitation of strange entities, which is certainly the aspect that provided much fuel to the Extra-Terrestrial Hypothesis (ETH). The reports of such entities constitute a relatively small percentage of UFO sightings, but it remains a long-lasting feature. The "visitations" of such entities tend to come in waves, which can be defined both in terms of the general appearances of the entities and their general behavior towards the witnesses. For instance, in the 1950s, a number of witnesses described having been contacted by friendly aliens from outer space; the witnesses came to be known as "contactees." Many reports of humanoid entities were produced in the 1970s, but there were much less of them in the 1980s, until a wave of UFO-related humanoid sightings hit the former Soviet Union in 1989-1990. In the 1990s, most reports were of the "abduction" type, where in many cases there was no sighting of a UFO in the sky, but the events were construed as being UFO-related.

Such waves in the type of "visitors" are both intriguing and suspicious. Some have interpreted these waves as the different time of arrival to Earth of various alien species, thus explaining similarities in reports. Although this may appear to be a simple and intuitive explanation of some extraordinary experiences reported by many witnesses, there is no solid evidence to support it. Others came to the conclusion that these waves are simply the result of social dynamics. Namely, one or a few persons have a strange experience that is interpreted in a particular way (e.g. an alien abduction) and then when others hear about it they also interpret their experiences the same way. With the larger diffusion offered by modern means of communication, this particular interpretation becomes a "truth" believed by many. Then the process repeats itself with a different content a few years later. This is a more complex and less intuitive explanation based on a sociological understanding of how social representations spread. This explanation is more satisfying as it takes into consideration a social reality relatively well understood in the social sciences. Unfortunately, it does so by excluding many hard to explain elements and details. Once again, how could we find a more satisfying explanation that does not come at the expense of ignoring many extraordinary witness' reports?

This chapter proposes to take a holistic look at these waves; it does not exclude what the witnesses had reported. In other words, social dynamics and extraordinary events are not necessarily mutually exclusive. Carl Jung in *Flying Saucers* adopts the same approach about UFO observations when he concluded that:

> Unfortunately, well-authenticated reports show that there are also cases where the eye sees something that does not appear on the radar screen, or where an object undoubtedly picked up by radar is not seen by the eye. I will not mention other, even more remarkable reports from authoritative sources; they are so bizarre that they tax our understanding and credulity to the limit.
>
> If these things are real—and by all human standards it hardly seems possible to doubt this any longer—then we are left with only two hypotheses: that of their *weightlessness* [immaterial aspects] on the one hand and their *psychic nature* on the other. This is a question I for one cannot decide.[314]

Although so-called alien encounters cannot be dismissed as mass hysteria or hallucination, as skeptics often claim they can, on the other hand they cannot be proven to be actual encounters in the physical sense of the word. In many ways, they seem to be something not fully objective and yet not fully subjective either. It is part of the class of phenomena that anthropologists call "liminal," i.e., those that are in-between two realms of reality.

Likewise, psi phenomena are also described as being liminal.[315]

The impersonal nature of the alien encounter

For the purpose of this chapter, a basic and yet instructive analysis of the interaction between the witnesses and the entities is proposed that goes beyond the usual explanations proposed for "alien" close encounters. The analysis uses the notion of power; namely, if this is an impersonal experience that is felt as being imposed on the witness, then power is being used. Power is defined in its simplest expression as the capacity to make someone do something that he or she would not do otherwise. The key questions raised in such a scenario are: Who is involved? How do they interact with each other? And what is the result of the interaction? The answers to those simple questions then lead to the identification of a limited set of qualitative variables. The first one identifies the key and typical social actors for each type of contact. For the sake of clarity, the analysis limits itself to two typical social actors: (a) aliens, and (b) witnesses/victims. The second variable looks at the nature of the power relationship between each actor, whether they are (a) relatively balanced or (b) unbalanced in favor of one side or the other. Two sub-variables are then necessary to qualify the nature of the relationship. The first sub-variable is the mode of expression, which describes how one can identify that power is in action. There are multiple examples, which include physical force, providing or denying knowledge, cooperation, confrontation etc. The second sub-variable is the focus of power, i.e. what is at stake. This is an important qualifier because it helps us to understand why the social actors behave as they do.

Using these criteria to analyze alien encounters, three types of "typical" contacts have been identified in the literature, and they can be described as: (a) space brothers, (b) abductors, and (c) terrorists (the frightening entities not engaging in abduction).

(a) The Space Brothers

The Space Brothers type is well illustrated with the life of individuals known as contactees, such as George Adamski,[316] George Van Tassel,[317] and many others not as well known.[318]

Since the first half of the 1950s, many books have been published recounting tales of contacts with alien beings. The time interval between the alleged contact and the publication of the book about it is usually a few years. Although there has been a long lull with very few new contactees in the last three decades, new contactees are now emerging. However, the contactee theme has remained part of our popular culture (e.g. Rael and the Raelians, the Heaven's Gate tragedy, etc) all this time. The evidence provided by contactees for their claims is flimsy; many logical flaws can be found in their descriptions. Their conversations with the entities are often quite naïve. For instance, a number of contactees described their visitors as coming from the planet Venus. We now know that Venus is an inferno, unlikely to sustain any evolved life forms. Contactees also have a long history of passing along "predictions" to humanity from the aliens, which in almost all instances either did not occur or were so vague that anything could be used as a "proof" that it occurred as predicted. Yet those who have investigated and met the contactees tend to believe that most of them appear to have experienced "something" quite unusual, even if the contactees ended up embellishing their stories afterward. Again, it is difficult to completely dismiss the contactees.

The usual actor in this type of contact is an ordinary person, having no special access to power or decision-making, and who is specifically selected and contacted by aliens to receive a message to be delivered to humanity. Human authorities are not active actors in this type of contact. Such messages are generally about the need for humans to establish world peace and create a kinder society, often with environment-friendly overtones. The messages are usually utopian in nature. Contacts with aliens are recounted as friendly and recurring. Importantly, many contactees tend to tell a story where they have one or more physical encounters at first, and then contact continues through the reception of telepathic messages.

When such an encounter is examined from an impersonal point of view, the underlying structure of such events can be described as follows: very powerful aliens who prefer to contact ordinary human beings, establishing a positive but fundamentally uneven relationship of power with the contactees. The alien power is expressed through teaching, i.e. creating a master–pupil type of relationship. Superior knowledge coming from elsewhere is transferred to us via a human messenger. The focus of power, i.e., the content of what is expected to change, is therefore about our present-day human social and political structure. The aliens want to see changes occurring in human societies through ordinary people. In this sense, the aliens indirectly defy human authorities by circumventing them and challenging their monopoly over social policy. The contactees become both empowered (i.e. increase their social status) by the knowledge provided by the aliens, but they can also lose social status by the ridicule they suffer afterward. To regain their lost social status, they must create a following, if not a cult, built around themselves.

(b) The Abductors

The abduction era "officially" started with the Barney and Betty Hill abduction in 1961, although the wider public did not learn of their story until 1966.[319] Yet the story of Villa-Boas in Brazil, who claimed to have been briefly abducted to have sexual intercourse with a female alien, predates the Hills' abduction by four years but became publically known in the English-speaking world in 1965 in an article in the *Flying Saucer Review*, a specialist publication with a small distribution.[320] The Andreasson case, in which Betty Andreasson claimed to have been abducted in her kitchen while the rest of her family was left in it in a "still" state, occurred in 1967 but the first in a series of books about the case was not published until 1979.[321] In the case of abductors, aliens are not friendly as they take people away against their will. They are described as uncaring when conducting medical examinations of their abducted victims. In most cases, the aliens appear to have a special interest in human reproductive organs. Evidence of this type of contact tends to be consistent across the globe, although they are often gathered through hypnotic regression, which is not thought to be a very reliable tool.[322] This type of contact has been more frequent since the late 1970s and continues to some extent to this day. The sheer number of abduction accounts makes them difficult to dismiss out of hand.[323]

The impersonal structure of events in the case of abductors is obvious. Again, it involves very powerful aliens, but this time they establish a negative and clearly unbalanced power relationship with the abductees. The alien power is being expressed by physical and mental control over the abductees. The focus of power is the reproductive capacity, particularly of the female. An alien more or less forces a human male to provide semen, or a human female is either providing eggs or is used as both breeder and biological incubator for alien-human hybrids. The abductees tend to lose credibility and social status if they make their stories public; they are often regarded as "crackpots" or mentally disturbed. To help in recalling the details of their abduction, they often end up seeing a ufologist who uses hypnosis, thus tainting significantly the story that emerges. This, in turn, may reinforce the alien nature of the experience for the abductee and, unfortunately, can isolate them socially even more.

(c) The Terrorists

The third type of alien contact resembles a terrorist intervention. In this case, the aliens are ugly and scary in appearance or violent in their behavior, or both. Descriptions of the entities tend to vary significantly from hairy monsters to reptilian aggressors. Evidence of this type of contact seems to come originally from South America. During the 1954 UFO wave, several reports from South America described terrifying aliens, either for their appearance or aggressive behavior.[324] Reports of that nature continue to this day if we include the infamous Chupacabras, which is often regarded as being an extraterrestrial entity.[325]

This type of contact presents an impersonal structure where ordinary people, i.e. not members of the elite, are terrified by aliens. The aliens establish an unbalanced relationship of power with the witnesses. The power relationship is expressed through terror. The focus of power in this type of contact is more difficult to assess. Alien terrorism is not leading to forced respect, obedience, or the elimination of curious people. Terror seems to be engendered for its own sake. The witnesses' social status appears to remain unchanged as they are usually seen as victims of some kind, usually of their own imaginations.

I have selected this typology of the space brother, abductor, and terrorist to show general patterns and tendencies. This does not mean that lies, hoaxes, embellishments, dreams, and hallucinations do not occur, but it means that the general weight of the evidence cannot be ignored. As well, there are other variations such as the so-called "Nordic" aliens that are very similar in the power structure we see in the Space Brother category. This typology also does not include many alien encounters that are more or less without a meaningful interaction; witnesses report strange people doing strange thing for a short time, but the "alien" does not pay attention to the witnesses. Of significance for this typology is the correlation that emerges between the articulation of the power relationships expressed through those different types of contacts with aliens and upcoming large-scale social changes that present similar relationships of power.

Type of Contact	Early Years	Future Social Context (date)	Expression of Power	Future Focus of Power	Alien interest / focus
Space Brothers	Early 1950s	Cultural Revolution (1960-70)	Teaching	Ordinary people together to peacefully educate others to create an utopian society	Utopian social and political changes through a messenger
Abductors	Early 1960s	Feminism (Late 1960s and on)	Physical and mental control	Women's control over own reproductive capacity	Interest in human reproductive systems, especially female
Terrorists	Early 1950s	State terrorism (1960-1990)	Terror	Maintaining power through violence and terror	Terror for its own sake

What this table shows are collective premonitions as seen through individual experiences. In other words, it appears as if social psi events get embedded into individual psi experiences. This could also be described as information reverberating through morphic resonance across fields, namely between the social and political fields and into the individual mental fields.

In the case of the space brothers, one can see the striking parallel with the Cultural Revolution of the 1960s. This period is marked by a significant shift in the attitudes towards formal authorities, and traditions. From the emergence of the pop culture and the hippies to the peace movement fueled by the Vietnam War, new social behaviors and worldviews were expressed, and many of them became the new "normal." The context of such expressions was essentially based on changing peacefully the mentality of those who maintained traditional attitudes. In other words, the young generation of the 1960s saw itself as being invested with a mission to change the world and to create a utopian society through social activism. Social change as the focus of power is nothing new in the Western world, but comprehensive and utopian social change leading to a social movement or Cultural Revolution built around non-economic struggles of sexuality, spirituality, fashion freedom, etc. was quite new then.

The abduction contacts show some interesting parallels with the rise of the feminist movement. The feminist movement of the late 1960s was different from any previous women's movement as it based most of its arguments and actions on women regaining control and power over their own reproductive capacity. In choosing when, and if, to have children, as well as how many, women could now decide for themselves to seek an education, to get a career, to become influential members of their community, to become politicians, etc. So not only were women regaining power over their own physical bodies, but they were regaining control over their own minds. Yet the focus of power remained fundamentally centered around reproductive capacities. The aliens in abducting and performing medical procedures on the abductees' reproductive system re-enacted symbolically the center point of power struggle that underpinned the feminist movement—but they did so *precognitively* as these abduction experiences occurred 5 to 7 years prior to the full-blown emergence of the feminist movement.

Lastly, the encounters with terrorizing aliens found in South America in the 1950s have striking parallels with the state-sponsored terrorism against its own citizens in the years that followed. Think about the systematic repression of opposition to aboriginal land claims by death squads, as well as the illegal arrests and unconstitutional tribunals and executions of suspected political opposition members. Terror became a way of ruling, an expression of power.

It is important to note that systematic state terrorism was totally new to South America when it appeared in the late 1950s, early 1960s. The Peron regime in Argentina, Pinochet in Chile, the military dictatorships in Brazil, Venezuela, Peru, etc., were all guilty of using terror as an instrument of power. It is important to understand that the use of terror was ultimately possible due to the extreme social inequalities found in those societies. A small ruling elite living in immense wealth was trying to stop any attempt to reduce its power and privilege. Widespread poverty and corruption encouraged many to either support Marxist-oriented guerillas or show civil resistance inspired by the Catholic Church clergy belonging to the theology of liberation. State terrorism became an end in itself and enemies were seen everywhere to the point of absurdity. For instance, simple roommates sharing an apartment in Chile were arrested on the pretext that what they were doing was a form of communism! Death squads eradicated villages so they wouldn't turn pro-guerilla, etc. In both cases, alien terrorism and state terrorism, terror became an end in itself. And again, terrorist alien contacts anticipated this excessive abuse of power used by many South American states by about 5 to 7 years.

Each type of alien encounter presents specific patterns of power relationships between aliens and humans. The same power relationship patterns emerge five to ten years later in major and historical social changes. It is always possible to say that those social changes were already in the making when the alien contacts occurred, but the vast majority of people involved in alien contacts can hardly be considered futurists or social scientists in tune with subtle changes in society.

These recurring anomalistic events involving "aliens" of various types seem to adopt and illustrate emerging social forms and structures at a point where they are still very much unconscious in their social representations. If this analysis is correct, then one has to acknowledge that alien encounters have a social meaning that goes beyond the individual experience of people who report encountering aliens. However, it tends to give credence to the idea that people who have had an alien encounter did actually have a very unusual experience beyond imagination and fantasy, but that something might be psi-based, covering both individual and social psi. On the other hand, it does not confirm in any way that those individual experiences are actual alien encounters. In fact, the enormous variety in settings and contexts, alien species, spacecraft involved, etc. — while involving a display of similar power patterns — are arguments against "flesh and blood" aliens. It appears, therefore, that alien encounters are like social mirrors or morphic reverberations across the physical and mental fields.

These kinds of "alien" encounters are continuing. But why do they do so long past what we might call their premonition stage? Perhaps the subsequent events can be regarded as reverberations of the same information in individual mental fields. Or perhaps they have new symbolic meanings to impart. A recent event comes to mind.

Blossom Goodchild, an Australian author and psychic, said that she had received a telepathic message from the "Federation of Light" that the aliens would finally make themselves visible and do something significant over a three-day period starting on October 14, 2008, in Alabama, forcing the government to take serious note and do a "real disclosure." Her story created quite a buzz at the time.[326]

As we all now know, no big ET show happened in Alabama or anywhere else for that matter. But a few days before the predicted date, on October 4, 2008 (just remove the "1" from the "14") a well-documented day sighting of *three* UFOs occurred in Philadelphia during a Bruce Springsteen concert, which was part of Barack Obama's campaign tour.[327] When Obama arrived at the stadium, the UFOs were gone, but he made history by becoming president exactly one month later. Could "Alabama" have been a misreading of "Obama?" Was Bruce singing "Blinded by the Light" at time of the UFO visit? These are the same kinds of "mistakes" or "misreadings" that remote viewers have been known to make in their psychic reading of remote people, places and things, according to parapsychologists.

The future of "alien encounters" is certainly hard to predict because there are so many elements and dynamics underlying it that we do not know or understand. However, it is probably safe to say that it is likely to evolve and morph over time as human affairs evolve and morph themselves. What seems clear, however, is that those "aliens" are in some way reflecting our own image, with possible precognitions of what is to come.

Conclusion

It's been more than a hundred years since the first UFO wave, the so-called Airship wave of the early 20th century, which was covered by the media, and almost seventy years since the first well publicized "flying saucer" story told by Kenneth Arnold. What we call the "UFO phenomenon" actually covers an array of diverse and enigmatic phenomena. It has been the hope of many since the late 1940s to find an answer to this enigma, but it resists explanation. The extraterrestrial hypothesis, which has driven interest in the phenomenon for much of this time, has brought us no closer to an understanding of the UFO subject. It is time to approach UFOs through a different lens, and I believe that the parapsychological approach is just such a lens.

While many researchers have noted the many paranormal aspects to the UFO phenomenon, they have tended to regard them as secondary effects and not as central to the phenomenon itself. I argue that the paranormal is actually the core of the phenomenon. Looking at UFO waves and UFO incidents as something akin to poltergeist disturbances is clearly challenging but also worthwhile. I think that by systematically integrating ideas and models from parapsychology into the study of UFOs we can get one step closer to making sense of the strangest aspects of the phenomenon. This new view provides us with a way to account for both the personal and impersonal dimensions without reducing one to the other.

Beyond providing a reasoned description of how a UFO wave or incident unfolds, the parapsychological approach encourages us to look into the symbolic dimension of the phenomenon. This is not an easy task because, as in any other study of the symbolic realm, whether literary, cultural, or dream analysis, it is open to interpretation. Yet applying this method of inquiry, however difficult, has shown some promise.

That's not to say that the parapsychological approach is the definitive answer to the UFO phenomenon. Parapsychological phenomena are themselves poorly understood. And psi, by definition, is not observable per se; only its effects are observable.

There is no observable direct cause-and-effect. Only indirect methods are available to us to understand how psi works—or how it might relate to the UFO phenomenon.

It is important to realize that psi phenomena are produced within a context of what sociologists call the social construction reality. What this means is that the actual experience is constructed based on our social and cultural assumptions. We see UFOs in the space age as we once saw ghost carriages in the pre-industrial era. Although some ufologists have noted the importance of social and cultural assumptions, they have rarely fully embraced its implications.

The parapsychological hypothesis I have presented here is based on the notion that truly enigmatic UFO events are psi-related. The implication of this hypothesis is that, ultimately, we are the ones producing UFOs, both as subjective projections of ourselves and as objective, but temporary, alterations of physical reality. This view has the definite advantage of being able to account for many aspects of UFO events that seem unrelated to one another, or appear to be absurd on the surface. The altered states of consciousness that many witnesses report during their encounters can now be viewed, as it is in parapsychology, as an enabling condition for the psi effects to occur, which if I am correct can apparently take the form of a UFO. With this understanding, just how physically objective the event is becomes somewhat less important, as psi events are ultimately symbolic events, whether at a personal or impersonal level, or both.

This approach frees us from the false choice of having to decide if the phenomenon is either subjective or objective, because it appears to actually be both at the same time. It also provides more flexibility in understanding the phenomenon because it allows for the subjective and the objective aspects to influence one another while existing in parallel. By removing this artificial barrier, this false either/or category, a wider perspective can be developed to embrace the full complexity of the phenomenon.

But this is by no means the end of the road. Far from closing the book on the UFO subject, the parapsychological hypothesis actually opens up many new and exciting ways of studying and researching not only the older cases but the new ones as well. Embracing this new look at an old enigma means that we will have a lot more questions than answers, but also that we will have new and, I think, better questions.

Acknowledgments

Writing a book on a controversial subject like the UFO phenomenon is a difficult task, fraught with risks of facing ridicule or being accused of committing heresies. Furthermore, to write one that argues against all the entrenched positions found in a controversy can be construed as pure folly. Yet, as in all debates on difficult subjects, the voice of the silent majority that simply tries to make sense of things is rarely heard. This book has been written for, and dedicated to, that silent majority who is not interested in defending a position but seeks to get a wider appreciation of a complex phenomenon.

Such a book, however, cannot be written alone. I received a lot help along the way from many people and appropriate thanks are in order. First, I would like to thank my blog readers who communicate their support and constructive criticism over the years. Their support helped me going on this difficult path of not espousing any particular strongly held position on the topic. I want also to thank some early supporters, like the French parapsychologist Dr. Renaud Everard and German physicist Dr. Walter von Lucadou. Their expert comments and suggestions helped me greatly in developing a better and more nuanced appreciation of anomalistic phenomena. I want also to thank Chris Laursen, historian of the paranormal, for our numerous discussions on the topic and for opening many doors along the way to various people and ideas.

In helping to shape this book, I would like to thank all the anonymous pre-readers for their comments and feedback. I would like also to offer my special appreciation for the comments and suggestions received from George Hansen, Dr. Jacques Vallée, and Robert Moore. Their views helped me to ensure that I remain in the narrow path between describing what is and proposing what could be.

I would like to extend by gratitude, in particular, to Ms. Susan Demeter for the research she has done to reinforce this book, her editorial support and the numerous corrections she proposed, her vast knowledge of the UFO phenomenon and contacts in the study of the paranormal, as well as her ongoing encouragements to keep me going in writing this book. I want also to express my thanks to Patrick Huyghe of Anomalist Books for his extensive comments and suggestions to improve this book and for believing in this project.

Finally, I would like to thank my partner in life, Monica Lelarge for her support, encouragements and for believing in this book. As well, I would like to give a special thank you to my three children for their patience while dad was busy working on this book.

In spite of all this support and help, any mistake, error, or omission that might have inadvertently found its way in this book is mine.

Glossary

Close Encounters Classification was first proposed in *The UFO Experience: A Scientific Study*, by J Allen Hynek, which was published in 1972. UFO sightings are put into two distinct categories; distant sightings and close encounters. The following lists the criteria for each classification within the close encounters category. Please note that close range usually means the UFO was estimated by the witness to be no more than 500 feet away.

Close Encounter of the First Kind CEI – A UFO seen at close range that has no interaction with the environment.

Close Encounter of the Second Kind CEII– A UFO seen at close range, and leaves physical traces or has physical effects on the witness or has some interaction with animals or objects.

Close Encounter of the Third Kind CEIII – A UFO seen at close range, and occupants are also observed.

Later additions to Hynek's classification for close encounters include the fourth and fifth kind

Close Encounter of the Fourth Kind CEIV – Abduction or contact, this can include any cases where witnesses experience a transformation of their sense of reality.

Close Encounter of the Fifth Kind CEV – An established communication.

Earthquake lights, also known sometimes by the term **earthlights,** are described as a luminous phenomenon that is at times seen in the sky at or near areas of tectonic stress, seismic activity, or volcanic eruptions.

Electromagnetism is a word scientists use to describe a wide range of phenomena associated with the behavior and interaction of electric currents and magnetic fields, such electromagnetic radiation.

ESP is the abbreviation for **extra-sensory perception,** which includes psychic phenomena such as telepathy, precognition, and clairvoyance.

ETH is the acronym for the **extraterrestrial hypothesis,** which is a popular attempted explanation for UFOs and humanoid contacts

Focus Person is a term used to denote someone that poltergeist phenomena appears to be centered around.

IFO stands for **identified flying object** and is used when a natural or mundane explanation is found for a UFO sighting report.

Morphic fields organize the form, structure, and patterned interactions of systems under their influence; including animals, plants, cells, proteins, crystals, brains and minds, societies, and cultures.

Morphic resonance relates to morphic fields. The morphic field resonates or transfers previous information or patterns through or across both space and time to a subsequent system of the same type.

MPI is the acronym for the **Model of Pragmatic Information**, which was developed by physicist and parapsychologist Walter von Lucadou. Von Lucadou noted that RSPK events go through four generic phases, where the phenomenon increases in intensity at the beginning until it peaks, and begins to decline, and finally disappears. These phases are labeled as surprise, displacement, decline, and suppression. The variations in the intensity of the psi events that are experienced are directly related to the types of people who become involved in the events.

MUFON is the acronym of the **Mutual UFO Network**, which is a primarily American-based civilian UFO investigation organization founded in the United States in 1969

The Nil Hypothesis proposes that all unsolved UFO reports would become IFOs if additional evidence became available. Statistical analyses on the differences between UFOs and IFOs such as those conducted by aerospace researchers in France provide a very strong challenge to this hypothesis.

OZ Factor is a term that was coined by UFO researcher Jenny Randles in her 1983 book, *UFO Reality*. It describes the altered states of consciousness reported by some UFO witnesses and experiencers of other types of paranormal phenomena. The witnesses' feelings of being in a slightly altered reality during their paranormal or UFO experience are likened to those experienced by characters in *The Wonderful Wizard of Oz* by L. Frank Baum while visiting the fairytale Land of Oz.

Parapsychology involves the experimental and quantitative study of psychic or psi phenomena. It is sometimes referred to as a sub-branch of psychology; however it is an interdisciplinary field involving people from various sciences.

PK is the abbreviation for **psychokinesis** which is the name given to psi or psychic phenomena that involve the ability of the mind to influence the physical environment such as objects moving seemingly on their own, electronic disturbances, and psychic healing. PK is also referred to as telekinesis or mind over matter.

Poltergeist is a word that comes from the German language and roughly translates to noisy ghost. In parapsychology, poltergeist phenomena are thought to be caused by spontaneous psychokinesis or RSPK.

Precognition is information about places or events before they occur.

Psi anomalous phenomenon studied by parapsychology. It is divided into two main categories ESP and PK and it suggests the possibility of causation of anomalous phenomena by mental processes.

RSPK is the acronym for **recurrent spontaneous psychokinesis,** which is quite literally spontaneous or unintentional psychokinesis that occurs over a period of time. RSPK is thought to be the causation in poltergeist disturbances.

Telepathy is considered to be the transfer of information, thoughts or feelings between individuals by means other than the five known senses.

UAP is the acronym for **unidentified aerial phenomenon,** which is a more accurate description of the various types of reported UFO phenomena. UFO sighting reports are often described as lights and not necessarily "objects." UAP is a preferred term amongst scientific UFOlogy.

UFOlogy is the study of UFOs.

UFO is the acronym for **unidentified flying object** a term first coined by the United States Air Force (USAF) in the early 1950s as a catch-all description for reports involving anomalies in the sky.

UFO Flap is a term used to describe reports of phenomena occurring in specific locations for an extended period. Generally speaking they are concentrated in a smaller area and of shorter overall duration than a UFO Wave.

UFO Wave is similar to a "UFO flap" these are noted by a marked increase in the number of UFO sightings over a period of time. UFO waves will build to a peak, and then begin to decreases until they reach a more typical number. Waves generally cover a much wider geographical area, and are of considerably longer duration than a "flap."

Reference Notes

Introduction

1 Vallée J, *UFOs: The Psychic Solution*, (St. Albans: Granada Publishing, 1977), 15. It was published in the United States in 1975 under the less explicit title of *The Invisible College* and reprinted under that title by Anomalist Books in 2014.

2 http://commons.wikimedia.org/wiki/File:Sierpinski_triangle_ (RGB).jpg, owner of this image granted to anyone the right to use this work for any purpose, without any conditions, unless such conditions are required by law.

3 Haines Gerald K. "CIA's Role in the Study of UFOs 1947-90," (accessed September 2014) https://www.cia.gov/library/center-for-the-study-of-intelligence/csi-publications/csi-studies/studies/97unclass/ufo.html

Section One: Studying UFOs

Chapter 1 What is known about UFOs

4 Rutkowski Chris and Geoff Dittman, "The Prime Minister and the UFO" in *The Canadian UFO Report: the Best Cases Revealed*, (Dundurn Press, 2006), 212-218. Please note that they did not provide the name of the airport to protect the identity of the government employees.

5 Keel John, "The people problem" in Spencer J. and H. Evans eds. *Phenomenon: Forty years of flying saucers* (New York: Avon Books, 1988) 186-198

6 United States, Air *Force Regulation No. 200-2* (Washington: Department of the Air Force 1954) 1 This document is available online at the NICAP website, accessed September 2014 http://www.nicap.org

7   Steiger Brad, *Project Blue Book*, (Ballantine Books, 1976) 214

8   Ibid 213

9   Project 1947 (accessed September 12, 2014) http://www.
project1947.com/articles/enclair.htm

10   Ridpath Ian, "Interview With J. Allen Hynek" *Nature*, Vol. 251
(October 1975) 369

Available on Internet at "Interview with J. Allen Hynek," (last modified
November 6, 2005) http://www.cohenufo.org/Hynek/hynk1975ridpath.
htm

11   For instance, Yousuo, Zou. "The Physical Explanation to the
UFO over Xinjiang, Northern West China." *Science of ball lightning
(fire ball)*. (1989): 273; Zou, Y. "The motion of wave energy and the
behavior of plasma fireball in the atmosphere." In *Plasma Science,
1997. IEEE Conference Record-Abstracts., 1997 IEEE International
Conference on*, p. 321. IEEE, 1997; Turner, D. J. (2003). The missing
science of ball lightning. *Journal of Scientific Exploration*, 17(3),
435-496; Bychkov, V. L., A. I. Nikitin, and G. C. Dijkhuis. "Ball
lightning investigations." In *The Atmosphere and Ionosphere*, pp. 201-
373. Springer Netherlands, 2010; Bychkov, Vladimir L., and Anatoly
I. Nikitin. "Ball Lightning: A New Step in Understanding." *The
Atmosphere and Ionosphere*. Springer International Publishing, 2014.
201-367.

12   Keel John, "Is the 'EM' effect a myth?" *Flying Saucer Review* 14,
no. 6 (1968)

13   Lagarde Ferdinand, *Flying Saucer Review* 14, no. 6 (1968)

14   Fort Charles, *New Land*. (New York: Boni & Liveright, 1923)

15   Lagarde Ferdinand, *Mystérieuses soucoupes volantes*, (Paris:
Étapes, 1973)

16   Strand Erling P. Project Hessdalen (accessed September 2014)
http://www.hessdalen.org/

17   Hauge, Bjørn Gitle. "Investigation & analysis of transient
luminous phenomena in the low atmosphere of Hessdalen valley,

Norway." *Acta Astronautica* 67.11 (2010): 1443-1450.

18   Clark J. "Interview with Jacques Vallée," in Curtis G Fuller Ed, *Proceedings of the First International UFO Congress*, (New York: Warner, 1980) 405

19   Forshufvud Ragnar, "UFO, ett fysykalist fenomen," *UFO-Sverige-Aktuellt* 1, no. 1 (1980)

20   Saidov M. S., "Macrofluctuating stable pinches in solar eruption plasma and the formation of a UFO". *Applied Solar Energy* June 2010, 46, 2, 138-141

21   Devereux Paul, *Earthlights* (Wellingborough: Turnstone Press 1982)

22   Persinger Michael A. "Geophysical models for parapsychological experiences," *Psychoenergetic Systems* 1 (1975) 63-74

— "ELF field mediation in spontaneous PSI events: direct information transfer or conditioned elicitation?," *Psychoenergetic Systems* 3 (1979) 155-169

— "Spontaneous telepathic experiences from Phantasms of the Living and Low Global Geomagnetic Activity," *Journal of the American Society for Psychical Research* 81 (1987) 23-36

— and Cameron R.A. "Are earth faults at fault in some poltergeist-like episodes?" *Journal of the American Society for Psychical Research* 80 (1986) 49-73

Schaut G.B and Persinger M.A., "Subjective telepathic experiences, geomagnetic activity and the ELF hypothesis: Part I. Data analyses." *PSI Research* 4, no. 1 (1985) 4-20

23   Persinger Michael A. and Lafrenière G.F. *Space-time Transients and Unusual Events* (Chicago: Nelson-Hall, 1977)

24   — "The tectonic strain theory as an explanation for UFO phenomena: A nontechnical review of the research, 1970-1990," *Journal of UFO Studies* 2 (1990) 105-137

— "The UFO experience: A normal correlate of human brain function," in *UFOs and Abductions: Challenging the borders of knowledge*, edited by David M. Jacobs (Lawrence: University Press of Kansas, 2000) 262-302

25   Budden Albert, *UFOs Psychic Close Encounters: The electromagnetic indictment* (London: Blandford, 1995) and *Electric Ufos: Fireballs, Electromagnetics and Abnormal States* (Darby: Diane Pub Co. 1998)

26   Partain Keith L. *Psi in the Sky: A new approach to UFO and psi phenomena* (Philadelphia: Xlibris 2001)

27   United Kingdom, *Unidentified Aerial Phenomena (UAP) in the UK Air Defence Region* (London: Ministry of Defence, 2000)

28   United Kingdom, *Unidentified Aerial Phenomena (UAP) in the UK Air Defence Region: Executive Summary* (London: Ministry of Defence, 2000), 12

29   Idem 7

30   Idem 7-8

31   Idem 9

32   "Unidentified Flying Objects -Project BLUE BOOK" See http://www.archives.gov/foia/ufos.html

33   Tennyson Rod, (2009) "The UTIAS UFO Project," *The UTIAS Newsletter* 2009 (2) 3 Available online at http://www.utias.utoronto.ca

34   "Aliens leave ADF cold." *Advertiser*, 22 November 1996, 8

35   "Resources cited as Britain closes unit that investigates UFO sightings," *National Post*. December 5 2009, A28

36   Duff Michelle, "Defence wants UFOs off its radar." *The Dominion Post*, 31 March 2011, A7

37   Healy Alison, "Irish UFOs blast into the light after 37 years in twilight zone," *The Irish Times* 20 September 2007 (accessed September 2014) http://www.ireland.com/newspaper/frontpage/2007/0920/1190238990654.html

38   Roussel Robert, "OVNI, la fin du secret" Belfond 1978

reproduced online (accessed September 2014) http://www.rhedae-magazine.com/OVNI-1976-la-position-officielle-de-l-armee-de-l-air-par-le-responsable-de-l-etude-du-phenomene_a716.html

39   Clas Svahn, "The Swedish Military UFO History," in Michael Sword and Robert Powell eds. *UFOs and Government: An Historical Inquiry*, (San Antonio: Anomalist Books, 2012) 371

40   De Brouwer Wilfred, "Postface." In SOBEPS, *Vague d'OVNI sur la Belgique: Un dossier exceptionnel.* (Bruxelles: SOBEPS), 491

41   Fuerza Aérea Uruguaya (accessed September 14 2014) http://www.fau.mil.uy/cridovni.html

42   Cardoso Rodrigo, "A história oficial dos ÓVNIS no Brasil," *Istoé Independente*, 22 July 2009, (accessed September 2014) http://www.istoe.com.br/reportagens/11862_A+HISTORIA+OFICIAL+DOS+OVNIS+NO+BRASIL

43   Comisión de Estudio de Fenómenos Aeroespaciales, *Fuerza Aérea Argentina* (accessed September 2014) http://www.fuerzaaerea.mil.ar/prensa/cefae.html

44   Kirby, D. "UFOs: Guatemala gripped by ET fever," *The Ottawa Citizen*, 5 March 1989, E4

45   Greenwood Barry J. and Bill Fawcett, *The UFO Cover-up*, (New York: Touchstone, 1990) 82

46   Kean Leslie, *UFOS, Generals, Pilots, and Government Records*, (New York: Three Rivers Press, 2010) 47

Chapter 2 Paranormal Research and UFOs

47   This story can be found in Scott Rogo, *The Haunted Universe*, (San Antonio: Anomalist, 2006) [Signet, 1977] 94

48   This story was fully investigated, and the witnesses were assessed by the psychiatrist Berthold Schwarz. Details are in his book *UFO Dynamics: Psychiatric and psychic aspects of the UFO syndrome.* (Moore Haven: Rainbow Books 1988) 140-149

49   Jung C.G, *Flying Saucers*, Trans by *R.F.C Hull* (New York: MJF 1978) 110

50   Ibid 111

51   Ridpath Ian, "Interview with J. Allen Hynek," *Nature*, Vol. 251 (October 4, 1975) 369

52   A copy of the letter can be found at http://psican.org/alpha/index. php?/20150411947/UFO-News-Articles-and-Editorials/Allen-Hynek-Comments-On-Toronto-Philip-Experiment.html

53   Clark Jerome and Loren Coleman, *The Unidentified*, (New York: Warner 1975) Reprinted in *The Unidentified & Creatures of the Outer Edge*, The Early Works of Jerome Clark and Loren Coleman, (San Antonio: Anomalist Books, 2006)

54   Ibid 242

55   Bearden, Thomas E. A *Mind/Brain/Matter Model Consistent with Quantum Physics and UFO phenomena*. Computer Sciences Corp Huntsville AL, 1979.

56   Rogo S, *The Haunted Universe*, 84

57   Randles Jenny, *UFO Reality: A Critical Look at the Physical Evidence* (London: R. Hale, 1983)

58   Cassirer Manfred, *Parapsychology and the UFO*, (London: n.p., 1988)

59   See: Partain Keith L. *Psi in the Sky: A new approach to UFO and psi phenomena*, (Philadelphia: Xlibris 2001), Budden Albert, *UFOs Psychic Close Encounters: The electromagnetic indictment*, (London: Blandford 1995), Hansen George P. *The Trickster and the Paranormal*, (Philadelphia: Xlibris 2001), Ouellet E. (2011). Social psi and parasociology, *Australian Journal of Parapsychology*, 11(1) 73-88

60   Noteworthy is a special issue on UFOs in the *Australian Journal of Parapsychology*, which includes the following: Basterfield, Keith and M.A. Thalbourne (2001) "Belief in, and Alleged Experience of, the Paranormal in Ostensible UFO Abductees" *Australian Journal of Parapsychology* 2(1): 2-18; Harvey-Wilson, Simon (2001) "Shamanism

and Alien Abductions: A Comparative Study,"— 103-116; Basterfield, Keith (2001) "Paranormal Aspects of the UFO Phenomenon: 1975-1999," *Australian Journal of Parapsychology* 1(1): 30-55

61   For more information please refer to their respective websites, Princeton Engineering Anomalies Research, (accessed September 2014) http://www.princeton.edu/~pear/ and

International Consciousness Research Laboratories, accessed September 2014, http://www.icrl.org/

62   R. G. Jahn, et al. (1997) "Correlations of Random Binary Sequences with Pre-Stated Operator Intention: A Review of a 12-Year Program," *Journal of Scientific Exploration*, Vol. 11, No. 3, pp. 345–367

63   Roll William G. (2003) "Poltergeists, Electromagnetism and Consciousness," *Journal of Scientific Exploration* 17, no. 1 75–86; and P. Brovetto and V. Maxia. (2008) "Some conjectures about the mechanism of poltergeist phenomenon," *NeuroQuantology* 6, no. 2, 1-8

64   Persinger Michael A. and S. A. Koren, "Predicting the characteristics of haunts from geomagnetic factors and brain sensitivity: Evidence from field and experimental studies," in Houran J. and Lange R. *Hauntings and poltergeists: Multidisciplinary perspectives*, (Jefferson: McFarland & Company, 2001) 179-194; and Roll William G. and M.A. Persinger, "Poltergeists and hauntings." in Houran and Lange, *Hauntings and poltergeists* 123-163

65   Heath Pamela Rae, *The PK Zone: A cross-cultural review of psychokinesis* (Lincoln: iUniverse, 2003)

Chapter 3 The Parapsychological Hypothesis

66   Vallée Jacques, *The Invisible College: What UFO Scientists Know about the Nature of Alien Influences on the Human Race*, (Penguin, 1977; Anomalist Books, 2014) 24

67   Ibid

68   John Keel, *The Cosmic Question*. (New York: Granada Publishing, 1978), 108

69   Portions of this chapter are drawn from a previous publication with the kind permission of the editor of the *Australian Journal of Parapsychology*. The original article is Eric Ouellet, "Social psi and parasociology." *Australian Journal of Parapsychology*. 11 (1) 73-88.

70   Radin Dean, *Entangled minds: Extrasensory experiences in a quantum reality*, (New York: Paraview 2006) 295

71   Fodor Nandor, *On the trail of the poltergeist*, (New York: Citadel Press 1958) 51

72   Rogo Scott, *Minds and motion: The riddle of psychokinesis*, (New York: Taplinger Publishing 1978) 195-196

73   Portions of this chapter are drawn from a previous publication with the kind permission of the editor of *EdgeScience*. The original article is Eric Ouellet, "Social Psi: A Framework for Understanding Large Scale Anomalies" *EdgeScience* 18 (June 2014). 5-11.

74   For a description of the poltergeist investigation done at the time see: Playfair Guy Lyon, *This House is Haunted: the True Story of a Poltergeist*, (London: Stein & Day, 1980)

75   Spencer John and A. Spencer, *The Poltergeist Phenomenon*, (London: Headline, 1997), 56

76   Ibid

77   Ibid 58

78   Dennett Michael, "A final interview with Milbourne Christopher" *Skeptical Inquirer* 9:2 (Winter 1984–85) 159–165

79   Playfair, *This House is Haunted*, 170

80   Brennan Zoe, "What IS the truth about the Enfield Poltergeist? Amazing story of 11-year-old London girl who 'levitated' above her bed," *Daily Mirror* 28 October 2011, (accessed September 2014) http://www.dailymail.co.uk/news/article-2054842/Enfield-Poltergeist-The-amazing-story-11-year-old-North-London-girl-levitated-bed.html

81   Nickell Joe, *The Science of Ghosts: Searching for Spirits of the Dead*, (Amherst: Prometheus Books, 2012)

82   For a good overview of the MPI please see Von Lucadou Walter and F. Zahradnik, "Predictions of the Model of Pragmatic Information about RSPK," *Proceedings of the Parapsychological Association Convention* 2004, available online (accessed September 2014) http://archived.parapsych.org/papers/09.pdf

83   For more general information on the MPI see: von Lucadou Walter, "The Model of Pragmatic Information MPI)," *European Journal of Parapsychology* 11 (1995): 58–75, and —, "The exo-endo-perspective of nonlocality in psycho-physical systems," *Cases, International Journal of Computing Anticipatory Systems* 2 (1998): 169– 185; and for how generic microphysics concepts can be extended to macroscopic events, see: Von Lucadou W. and H. Römer and H. Walach, "Synchronistic phenomena as entanglement correlations in generalized quantum theory," *Journal of Consciousness Studies*, 14(4) (2007): 50–74

84   Heath P. R. *The PK zone: A cross-cultural review of psychokinesis*, (Bloomington, IN: iUniverse 2003), and Von Lucadou W. and F. Zahradnik, (2004), "Predictions of the Model of Pragmatic Information about RSPK," In *Proceedings of the 47th Annual Convention of the Parapsychological Association* (Durham, NC: Parapsychological Association 2004) 99-112

85   Roll William, *The Poltergeist*, (New York: Paraview 1972) [2004] and Roll, W. G. & M. A Persinger, (2001), "Poltergeists and hauntings," in Houran and Lange, eds. *Hauntings and poltergeists* 123-163

86   Eisenbud J, *Parapsychology and the unconscious*, (Berkeley, CA: North Atlantic Book 1983)

87   Fodor Nandor, *On the trail of the poltergeist*, (New York: Citadel Press 1958) and Von Lucadou, and Zahradnik, *Predictions of the Model of Pragmatic Information about RSPK*

88   Aimé Michel, *"About Flying Saucers"* (*"Mystérieux objects célestes"*), ed. Arthaud, 1958

89   A more detailed discussion of the French UFO wave of 1954

can be found in Ouellet E. "Social Psi and Parasociology," *Australian Journal of Parapsychology* 11 (1) (2011): 73–88

90   D. A. Johnson, (2009) The Worldwide UFO wave of 1954, retrieved June 3, 2011 from: http://www.nicap.org/reports/waveof1954. htm

91   Zervoudakis A. (2002) "A case of successful pacification," in Alexander M. and J. F. V. Keiger eds. *France and the Algerian War: Strategy, operations and diplomacy* (London: Frank Cass) 54-64

92   Pickles D. (1961) "The seven-year struggle in Algeria: Retrospect and prospect." *The World Today*, 17 (11) 479-489

93   Girardet R. *La crise militaire française 1945-1960: Aspects sociologiques et idéologiques*, (Paris: Armand Colin 1964)

94   Kripal, J. J, *Authors of the Impossible: The paranormal and the sacred*, (Chicago: Chicago University Press 2010) 25.

Section Two : Explaining UFO Anomalies

Chapter 4 Washington DC UFO Wave

95   This chapter is a slightly modified version of an article published in the *Australian Journal of Parapsychology*. It is reproduced with the kind permission of the editor. The original article is Ouellet E. "Extending von Lucadou's Model of Pragmatic Information to UFOs: A case study of the 1952 Washington DC UFO Wave." *Australian Journal of Parapsychology*, 11 (2), 116-137.

96   Hynek J Allen, *The Hynek UFO report*, (New York: Dell 1977) 264

97   Ibid 263

98   The National Investigations Committee On Aerial Phenomena (NICAP) (accessed September 2014) http://www.nicap.org/

99   Von Lucadou W, and F. Zahradnik, "Predictions of the Model of Pragmatic Information about RSPK," in *Proceedings of the 47th Annual Convention of the Parapsychological Association* (Durham,

NC: Parapsychological Association. 2004) 100

100   Randle K. *Invasion Washington: UFOs over the Capitol* (New York: HarperCollins 2001) 39

101   Ibid

102   Carlson Peter, (2002) "Alien Armada! 50 Years Ago, Unidentified Flying Objects From ..." *Washington Post*, (21 July) F01

103   Randle, *Invasion Washington* 34

104   Ibid 39

105   Von Lucadou and Zahradnik, "Predictions of the Model of Pragmatic Information about RSPK," 100

106   Randle, *Invasion Washington*, 70

107   Ibid 68-74

108   Carlson, "Alien Armada! 50 Years Ago, Unidentified Flying Objects"

109   Von Lucadou and Zahradnik, "Predictions of the Model of Pragmatic Information about RSPK," 100

110   Randle, *Invasion Washington: UFOs over the Capitol*, 31

111   Von Lucadou and Zahradnik, "Predictions of the Model of Pragmatic Information about RSPK," 101

112   Ibid 105

113   Randle, *Invasion Washington*, 32-74

114   "Television in Smoke-filled Rooms," *The Economist*, 19 July 1952, 166

115   Von Lucadou and Zahradnik, "Predictions of the Model of Pragmatic Information about RSPK," 103

116   Ibid

117   Schrecker Ellen, *The Age of McCarthyism*. (New York: Palgrave,

2002), 43-47

118 Jung C.G. *Flying Saucers* Trans by *R.F.C Hull* (New York: MJF 1978), 136

Chapter 5 Belgian Wave

119 Bougard Michel and Lucien Clerebaut, "Chronique d'une vague," in *SOBEPS, Vague d'OVNI sur la Belgique: Un dossier exceptionnel,* (Bruxelles: SOBEPS, 1991) 51

120 Ibid 260-279

121 Ibid 82

122 Copyright SOBEPS: Vague d'OVNI sur la Belgique - Une énigme non résolue, 1994. (accessed September 2014) http://www. cobeps.org/fr/vague_belge.html. Used with Permission

123 Bougard and Clerebaut, "Chronique d'une vague," 150

124 Boitte Franck, (2012). "Belgian Ufology: What Future Developments Are To Be Expected After The Petit-Rechain Fiasco?" (accessed September 2014) www.cobeps.org/pdf/belgian_wave_130310.pdf

125 Ibid 78

126 Ferryn, "Vidéofilms et photographies," in *SOBEPS, Vague d'OVNI sur la Belgique: Un dossier exceptionnel,* (Bruxelles: SOBEPS.1991) 397

127 "Famous Belgian UFO photo a hoax," CAELESTIA, (accessed September 2014) http://www.caelestia.be/article05ad.html

128 Ferryn, "Vidéofilms et photographies," 414

129 Meessen Auguste, "Les observations décisives du 29 novembre 1989," in *SOBEPS, Vague d'OVNI sur la Belgique: Un dossier exceptionnel,* (Bruxelles: SOBEPS 1991a) 25

130 Ibid 25-27

131 Ibid 16

132 Ibid 16-18

133 Ibid 23-24

134 Ibid 20-47

135 Bougard and Clerebaut, "Chronique d'une vague," 69

136 Ibid 82-113

137 Ibid 90-92

138 Ibid 180

139 Ibid 226

140 Ibid 181

141 Ibid 226

142 Ibid 182-184

143 Ibid 226

144 Ibid 226

145 Ibid 227-228

146 "Report concerning the observation of UFOs in the night
from March 30 to March 31, 1990" UFO Evidence, English version
(accessed September 2014) http://www.ufoevidence.org/documents/
doc408.htm

147 Bougard and Clerebaut, "Chronique d'une vague," 259-282

148 Ibid 280

149 Ibid 278

150 Ibid 94-106

151 Ibid 84-85

152 Lambrechts Report, (accessed September 2014) http://www.

ufoevidence.org/documents/doc408.htm

153   Meessen Auguste, "La détection radar," in SOBEPS, *Vague d'OVNI sur la Belgique: Un dossier exceptionnel*, (Bruxelles: SOBEPS,1991b) 364-365

154   De Brouwer Wilfried, "Postface," in SOBEPS, *Vague d'OVNI sur la Belgique: Un dossier exceptionnel*, (Bruxelles: SOBEPS 1991) 489

155   Bougard and Clerebaut, "Chronique d'une vague," 52-62

156   Ibid 118-122

157   Ibid 123

158   Ibid 73

159   Ibid 79

160   Ibid 78

161   Ibid 122

162   Ibid 125-126

163   Ibid 143

164   Ibid 144-145

165   Ibid 77 and 113

166   Ibid 114-115

167   Ibid 140

168   Ibid 126

169   "Histoire du Radar," Patrimonium, Histoire de Fexhe et Slins, (accessed September 2014) http://fexhe-slins-patrimonium.weebly. com/radar-de-glons.html

169b Vallee Jacques, *UFO Chronicles of the Soviet Union: A Cosmic Samizat*, (Ballantine Books, 1992)

170   The CIA doubted of the relevance of NATO in the National

Intelligence Estimate, "The Future of Eastern Europe – Key Judgements," *Langley: Central Intelligence Agency*, April 1990, p. vii. Similarly, in the *NATO Review*, Vol. 38- No. 2 April 1990, p. 16 – 23, it was already openly discussion the existential challenges of the organization. Discussions about German unification raised the issue of the need for Germany to remain a member of NATO, web page (accessed September 2014) http://hansard.millbanksystems.com/commons/1990/apr/03/german-unification

171 Copyright NATO. Image used in accordance to NATO's copyright standard permission and rules.

Chapter 6 Rendlesham Forest Incident

172 Digital copies of these reports can be found on a number of websites, including the one maintained by Ian Ridpath , (accessed September 2014) http://www.ianridpath.com/ufo/rendlesham.htm

173 Police reports are available online on the Suffolk Constabulary website, (accessed September 2014) http://www.suffolk.police.uk/aboutus/yourrighttoinformation/freedomofinformation/publicationscheme/idoc.ashx?docid=8639184b-b8fe-40ed-9b8c-932bd724e1c4&version=-1

174 Ridpath Ian, Rendlesham (accessed September 2014) http://www.ianridpath.com/ufo/rendlesham.htm

175 Rayl A.J.S. "Into The Night" Omni Project: Open Book available through the internet archive http://web.archive.org/web/19970607031756/www.omnimag.com/open_book/bent11.html

176 Easton James, "Rendlesham Revelations" *Fortean Times*, (accessed September 2014) http://www.forteantimes.com/features/articles/257/rendlesham_revelations.html

177 Clarke David, "New Light on Rendlesham" (accessed September 2014) http://drdavidclarke.co.uk/secret-files/secret-files-4/

178 Ibid

179 See http://devoid.blogs.heraldtribune.com/15233/did-va-just-

confirm-ufo-dangers/

180   United Kingdom, *Unidentified Aerial Phenomena (UAP) in the UK Air Defence Region*, Vol. 2, Annex F (London: Ministry of Defence, 2000), 4

181   Heazell P. *Most Secret: The Hidden history of Orford Ness*, (Stroud: The History Press 2010)

182   "Orford Ness," Global Security.org, accessed September 2014 http://www.globalsecurity.org/wmd/world/uk/orford_ness.htm

183   "1980: Government announces missile sites," *On This Day In History BBC News* (accessed September 2014) http://news.bbc.co.uk/onthisday/hi/dates/stories/june/17/newsid_2514000/2514879.stm

184   Edwards Rob, "US deployed nuclear weapons in the UK despite warning," *Science Direct*, DOI: 10.1016/S0262-4079(07)61745-X http://www.sciencedirect.com/science/article/pii/S026240790761745X

185   A.W.R.E, (1980) *"Plutonium dispersion aspects of GLCM storage – revise assessment,"* December 1980, DGV/80/S.C/300, 2 December 1980

186   Barnett Antony, "The timebomb that threatens Britain" *The Observer*, Sunday 24 October 1999, (accessed September 2014) http://www.theguardian.com/uk/1999/oct/24/theobserver.uknews5

187   The Redfern Inquiry: into human tissue analysis in UK nuclear facilities, Volume 1: Report, United Kingdom, 16 November 2010, (accessed September 2014) 379 https://www.gov.uk/government/uploads/system/uploads/attachment_data/file /229155/0571_i.pdf

188   Van De Castlea R. L., (1969). "The Facilitation of ESP through Hypnosis," *American Journal of Clinical Hypnosis* (Volume 12, Issue 1), 37-56

189   Picture of hand reproduction of Penniston's drawing by the author of this book.

190   Copyright free picture, including modifications, granted by HardingPhotography.co.uk, under the Creative Commons Attribution 3.0 License. Copyright information is available at http://en.wikipedia.

org/wiki/File:Greenham_Common_New_Sign.JPG

191   Heazell, *Most Secret: The Hidden history of Orford Ness*

192   A.W.R.E, (1980), *"Plutonium dispersion aspects of GLCM storage – revise assessment"*

193   Ibid

194   http://www.qtm.net/~geibdan/a1999/cash3.htm.

195   http://www.who.int/mediacentre/factsheets/fs371/en/.

196   http://www.bt.cdc.gov/radiation/arsphysicianfactsheet.asp

197   http://www.who.int/peh-emf/meetings/archive/en/keynote3ng.pdf

Section Three: Complex UFO Encounters

Chapter 7 Canadian Wave

198   Magor John, "1967 Canadian UFO Wave: The Year We Were Invaded Without Knowing It" UFO Evidence, (accessed September 2014) http://www.ufoevidence.org/documents/doc683.htm

199   Expression used by Richard H. Hall, and echoed by the Karl T. Pflock in a book review in the *Journal of Scientific Exploration*, (accessed September 2014) http://www.scientificexploration.org/journal/reviews/reviews_18_4_pflock_2.pdf

200   Keel John, "North America 1966: Development of a Great Wave," *Flying Saucer Review*, Vol. 13, 2, Mar.-Apr. 1967

201   Hall Richard H. "1967: The Overlooked UFO Wave and The Colorado Project," *MUFON 1978 UFO Symposium Proceedings*, 51-74 available online, (accessed September 2014) http://www.nicap.org/papers/78hall-wave67.htm

202   Sheldrake Rupert, "Morphic Fields and Morphic Resonance," *Noetic Now*, (accessed September 2014) http://www.noetic.org/noetic/issue-four-november-2010/morphic-fields-and-morphic-resonance/

203 "Canada's UFOs: The Search for the Unknown," Library and Archives Canada, (accessed September 2014) http://www. collectionscanada.gc.ca/ufo/002029-2501-e.html

204 Hall Richard H. "Alien Invasion of Human Fantasy? The 1966-67 UFO wave," (Washington: Fund for UFO Research 2004)

205 Accessible online at Library and Archives Canada, (accessed September 2014) http://www.collectionscanada.gc.ca/ufo Also available through Canadian X-Files (accessed September 2014) at http://ufo-joe.tripod.com which provides a useful index to search the government database.

206 UFO DNA: Breaking the UFO Code, available only through the internet archive http://www.ufodna.com

207 Water UFO.net, accessed September 2014 http://www.waterufo. net

208 The Hynek classification for close encounters (CE) is divided in three sub-groups. The first kind (CE1) when someone sees an object from up close, the second kind (CE2) when physical traces are left behind; and the third kind (CE3) when witnesses see or interact with UFO occupants.

209 For a detailed account of projects Magnet and Second Storey, please refer to Arthur Bray, *The UFO Connection*, (Ottawa: Jupiter Publishing 1979)

210 "Canada's UFOs: The Search for the Unknown" Library and Archives Canada, (accessed September 2014) http://www. collectionscanada.gc.ca/ufo/002029-2401-e.html

211 — http://www.collectionscanada.gc.ca/databases/ufo/001057-119.02-e.php?isn_id_nbr=4668&page_id_nbr= 82&record_id=4668-82-7093&interval=20&PHPSESSID=3k4si42dsmblct491dsi7p1fq3

212 — http://www.collectionscanada.gc.ca/databases/ufo/001057-119.02-e.php?isn_id_nbr=4668&page_id_nbr= 79&record_id=4668-79-7090&interval=20&PHPSESSID=589dsmqutk9qbl8ohmoso73aa1

213 —http://www.collectionscanada.gc.ca/databases/ufo/001057-119.02-e.php?isn_id_nbr=4668&page_id_nbr= 84&record_id=4668-

84-7095&interval=20&PHPSESSID=t4n0ms84tg2u5vvfu38fs2u313

214   UFO DNA: Breaking the UFO Code, available only through the internet archive http://www.ufodna.com/ufl3/uf7/137861.htm

215   Ibid

216   Rosales Albert S. "Humanoid Sighting Reports & Journal of Humanoid Studies," (accessed September 2014) http://www.ufoinfo.com/humanoid/humanoid1967.shtml

A RCMP police report is quoted as the original source.

217   Creston, The Alien Digest Vol. 4, (accessed September 2014) http://www.projectcamelot.org/Alien_Digest_Vol_4.pdf

218   Canadian X-Files (accessed September 2014) http://ufojoe.tripod.com/books/gateway116caldonia.html

219   UFO DNA: Breaking the UFO Code available only through the internet archive http://www.ufodna.com/uf10/uf3/103395.htm

220   Tokarz Harry, "UFO Witnesses, Public Property?" MUFOB new series 11, Summer 1978 Available online, (accessed September 2014) http://magonia.haaan.com/2009/property/

221   Rojcewicz Peter M. (1987) "The 'Men in Black' experience and tradition: Analogues with the traditional devil hypothesis," *Journal of American Folklore* 100 (396): 148-160

222   Eisenbud Jule, *Parapsychology and the Unconscious*, (Berkeley: North Atlantic Book 1983)

223   Rouse Wayne R. and John G. McCutcheon (1970)"The effect of the regional wind on air pollution in Hamilton, Ontario," *Canadian Geographer* 14(4): 271-285

224   "Industrial Hamilton: a trail to the future, Stelco, Incorporated (The Steel Company of Canada), Library and Archives Canada, (accessed September 2014)

http://epe.lac-bac.gc.ca/100/205/301/ic/cdc/industrial/stelcomain.htm

225   The Steel Making Industry, (accessed September 2014) http://

www.istc.illinois.edu/info/library_docs/manuals/primmetals/chapter2.
htm

226   Stelco R & D, accessed September 2014 http://stelcoresearch.
blogspot.com/2008/09/opening-of-stelco-research-centre.html

227   History of Industry in Hamilton, (accessed September 2014)
http://epe.lac-bac.gc.ca/100/205/301/ic/cdc/industrial/history.htm,and
Timeline of Hamilton Industry, (accessed September 2014)

http://epe.lac-bac.gc.ca/100/205/301/ic/cdc/industrial/timeline1979.
htm

228   Shag Harbour, UFO Evidence, (accessed September 2014)
http://www.ufoevidence.org/Cases/CaseSubarticle.asp?ID=179

229   UFO DNA: Breaking the UFO Code available only through the
internet archive, http://www.ufodna.com/uf10/uf1/101169.htm

230   Sudbury In The 1960s, (accessed September 2014) http://www.
thesudburystar.com/ArticleDisplay.aspx?archive=true&e=1270773

231   Berton Pierre, 1967, *the Last Good Year* (Doubleday Canada; 1st
Edition September 2, 1997)

232   Ibid

233   Rosales Albert S. "Humanoid Sighting Reports & Journal of
Humanoid Studies," (accessed September 2014) http://www.ufoinfo.
com/humanoid/humanoid1967.shtml This is based on Saucers, Space
& Science, Fall 1968

234   — http://www.ufoinfo.com/humanoid/humanoid1967.shtml

This is based on a newspaper article from the *Moncton Times*, August
17, 1967.

235   — http://www.ufoinfo.com/humanoid/humanoid1967.shtml

A RCMP police report is quoted as the original source.

236   — http://www.ufoinfo.com/humanoid/humanoid1967.shtml,
John Brent Musgrave, *UFO occupants and critters: The patterns in
Canada*, (N.L.: Global Communications, 1979) is quoted as the

source, but Musgrave does not provide his own sources.

237 Ibid

238 — http://www.ufoinfo.com/humanoid/humanoid1967.shtml

This is based on a local police report, and was investigated by APRO. The APRO report is likely to be unavailable for further information

239 "Canada's UFOs: The Search for the Unknown" Library and Archives Canada, (accessed September 2014) http://www. collectionscanada.gc.ca/ufo/002029-2502-e.html

240 — copy of the original, http://www.collectionscanada.gc.ca/ ufo/002029-2502.01-e.html

241 Rutkowski Chris, and Geoff Dittman, *The Canadian UFO Report: The best cases revealed,* (Toronto: Dundurn Press, 2006) 77

242 Peel Bruce, "FALCON, PIERRE," in Dictionary of Canadian Biography, vol. 10, University of Toronto/Université Laval, 2003, (accessed September 18, 2014) http://www.biographi.ca/en/bio/falcon_ pierre_10E.html

243 "La chanson des Bois-Brûlés," Centre du patrimoine, (accessed September 18, 2014) http://shsb.mb.ca/node/374

244 Uranium in Canada, World Nuclear Association, (accessed September 2014) http://www.worldnuclear.org/info/inf49.html

245 "Canada's UFOs: The Search for the Unknown" Library and Archives Canada, (accessed September 2014) http://www. collectionscanada.gc.ca/ufo/002029-1200.01-e.html

246 — original copy http://www.collectionscanada.gc.ca/ufo/002029- 2502.02-e.html

247 Alberta Genweb http://www.rootsweb.ancestry.com/~abcamros/ and Alberta's Francophone Heritage Infokit, this is an accessible, but archived page (accessed September 2014) http://www.edukits.ca/ francophone/en/elementary/infomania_text_french.html

248 From Fondation René-Lévesque, "Projet de lettre adressée à Jean Lesage (2 août 1967)," (accessed September 2014) http://

fondationrene-levesque.org/documentation/ecrits-de-rene-levesque/
textes/projet-de-lettre-adressee-a-jean-lesage-2-aout-1967/

249   Rutkowski, and Dittman, *The Canadian UFO Report*, 94

250   "Canada's UFOs: The Search for the Unknown," Library
and Archives Canada, (accessed September 2014) http://www.
collectionscanada.gc.ca/ufo/002029-2502.03-e.html

251   — http://www.collectionscanada.gc.ca/databases/ufo/001057-
119.02-e.php?isn_id_nbr=4669&page_id_nbr=204&record_id=4669-
204-7193&interval=20&PHPSESSID=furspoo0jlegq3khtpfc446k22

252   For a detailed account of this case, please refer to Don
Ledger, and Chris Styles, *Dark Object: The world's only government
documented UFO crash*. (New York: Dell 2001)

253   Ibid 13-27

254   UFO DNA: Breaking the UFO Code, available only through the
internet archive http://www.ufodna.com/uf05/uf6/056206.htm

Chapter 8 The Barney and Betty Hill Story Revisited

255   Fuller J. G. *The Interrupted Journey*. (New York: Medallion,
1966) 28

256   Fuller, *The Interrupted Journey* 213

257   Hall Richard H. (1979) "Hill Radar-UFO Connection Weak,"
MUFON UFO Journal No.140 (accessed January 2 2009) http://www.
nicap.org/hillradarweak.htm available through the internet archive

258   Ibid 267

259   Teodorani, Massimo (2004) "A Long-Term Scientific Survey of
the Hessdalen Phenomenon," *Journal of Scientific Exploration* No.
18(2) 217-251, 232-233.

260   Heath, *The PK zone* 220-222

261   Randles Jenny, *UFO reality: A critical look at the physical*

evidence, (London: R. Hale 1983)

262 — (2004), "View from Britain," *MUFON UFO Journal No. 432* April 04 18-19

263 Fuller, *The Interrupted Journey*. 125-127

264 Ibid 184

265 Heath, *The PK zone* 316-320

266 Fuller, *The Interrupted Journey* 121

267 Heath, *The PK zone* 256

268 Ibid 258

269 Fuller, *The Interrupted Journey* 253

270 Ibid 283

271 Ibid

272 Heath, *The PK zone* 266

273 Ibid 307

274 Spanos N. P. et al. (1993) "Close encounters: An examination of UFO experiences," (*Journal of Abnormal Psychology* 102) 624-632, and Basterfield K. and Thalbourne, M. A. (2002) "Belief in, and alleged experience of, the paranormal in ostensible UFO abductees," (*Australian Journal of Parapsychology*, 2) 2-18

275 Heath, *The PK zone* 314

276 Fuller, *The Interrupted Journey* 243-244

277 Schwarz B.E. *UFO dynamics: Psychiatric and psychic aspects of the UFO syndrome*, (Moore Haven, FL: Rainbow 1983) 273-281

278 Friedman Stanton and Kathleen Marden, *Captured! The Betty and Barney Hill UFO Experience* (Franklin Lakes, NJ: New Page Books, 2007) 211-218

279 Fuller, *The Interrupted Journey*, 33, 101, and 108

280   Ibid 319

281   Ibid 232

282   Ibid 39

283   Ibid

284   Ibid 49 and 71

285   Ibid 41

286   Ibid 46

287   Ibid 50

288   Ibid 62-65

289   Ibid 72

290   Ibid 69

291   Ibid 178

292   Ibid 94

293   Ibid 97

294   Ibid 114

295   Ibid 115

296   See the " Introduction" written in 1966 by Dr. Benjamin Simon, in John Fuller's *The Interrupted Journey* (New York: Berkeley Publishing) 5

297   See in particular his famous book: Frantz Fanon, *"Black Skin, White Masks"* Trans. Charles L. Markmann (USA: Grove Press 1967) [1952]

298   Kottmeyer Martin, (1996) "UFO Flaps," *The Anomalist* 3 (1995-1996): 64-89; and

Pierre Viéroudy, *Ces ovnis qui annoncent le surhomme*, (Paris: Tchou 1977)

299   NIE 11-8/1-61 – "Strength and Deployment of Soviet Long Range Ballistic Missile Forces," 21 September 1961 (29 pages), (accessed December 22, 2008) http://www.milnet.com/cia/nies/1961.htm

For more information please refer to Blechman Barry M. and Stephen S. Kaplan, *Force Without War*, (Washington: Brookings Institution Press 1978)

300   For more information on the Freedom Ride please refer to Arsenault Raymond, *Freedom Riders: 1961 and the Struggle for Racial Justice*. (Oxford: Oxford University Press 2006)

301   Anderson Benedict, *Imagined Communities—Reflections on the Origins and Spread of Nationalism*. (London: Verso 1983)

302   Copyright University of New Hampshire. University of New Hampshire's special collection Collection number: MC 197. Used with permission.

303   Copyright Alden Jewell. Used under Creative Commons Attribution 2.0 Generic License. Information on license available at https://www.flickr.com/photos/autohistorian/5129792982/

304   Courtesy United States Library of Congress's Prints and Photographs division under the digital ID cph.3b42416

305   Copyright Sue Demeter. Used with permission.

306   Fuller, *The Interrupted Journey*, 196

307   Ibid 316-317

308   Ibid 317-318

309   For more information please see LOVING v. VIRGINIA, 388 U.S. 1 (1967) Full text available online, (accessed September 2014) http://laws.findlaw.com/us/388/1.html

310   Fuller, *The Interrupted Journey* 208-209

311   Friedman, and Marden, *Captured!*

312   Copyright free picture, including modifications, granted by

Zeta_reticuli.png: en:User:Clementi, under the Creative Commons
Attribution-Share Alike 2.5 Generic license. Copyright information is
available at http://commons.wikimedia.org/wiki/File:Zeta_reticuli.svg

313 Courtesy the United States Library of Congress Geography and
Map Division, 0904003r.

Chapter 9 The Political Sociology of Alien Encounters

314 Jung C.G. *Flying Saucers* Trans by *R.F.C Hull* (New York: MJF
1978) 109

315 Hansen George P. *The trickster and the paranormal*,
(Philadelphia, PA: Xlibris 2001)

316 Leslie D. and G. Adamski, *Flying Saucers Have Landed*,
(London: Thomas Werner Laurie 1953)

317 Van Tassel G. W. *I Rode a Flying Saucer!* (Los Angeles: New
Age Publishing 1952)

318 Redfern Nick, *Contactees: A History of Alien-Human Interaction*,
(Pompton Plains, NJ: Career Press 2009)

319 Fuller J. G. *The Interrupted Journey*, (New York: Medallion,
1966)

320 Creighton G. "The amazing case of Antonio Villas Boas," in
Scott Rogo ed. *UFO Abductions: True cases of alien kidnapping*, (New
York: Signet 1980) 51 -85

321 Fowler Raymond, The *Andreasson Affair*, (Englewood Cliffs:
Prentice-Hall 1979)

322 McNally Richard J. (2012) "Explaining "memories" of space
alien abduction and past lives: An experimental psychopathology
approach," *Journal of Experimental Psychopathology* 3 (1): 2-16.

323 Bryan C.D.B. *Close Encounters of the Fourth Kind: Alien
abduction, UFOs, and the conference at M.I.T.* (New York: Knopf
1995)

324 Lorenzen Coral, *Flying Saucers: The startling evidence of
the invasion from outer space*. (New York: Signet 1962) 44-55, and

Creighton G. (1966) "The Humanoids in Latin America," *Flying Saucer Review - Special Issue* (October-November) 30-46

325   Corrales Scott, *Chupacabras and Other Mysteries*, (Austin: Greenleaf Publications 1997)

326   Wuttunee Stephane, "Blossom Goodchild's Predicted Mass UFO Sighting: Will it Force Disclosure to Occur?" UFO Digest, posted September 8, 2008 (accessed September 2014) http://www.ufodigest. com/news/0908/blossom.html

327   "UFOs over Philly during Bruce Springsteen/Obama concert," uploaded on 6 Oct 2008 by user juno2070, (accessed September 2014) https://www.youtube.com/watch?v=Qi5Wmby9dSE See also "UFO sighting over Philly?," ABC Action News, October 8, 2008, (accessed September 2014)   http://6abc.com/archive/6438701/

Bibliography

Alexander John. *UFOs: Myths, Conspiracies, and Realities*. St. Martin's Griffin 2012.

A.W.R.E. *"Plutonium dispersion aspects of GLCM storage – revise assessment." December 1980.* DGV/80/S.C/300. 2 December 1980.

ABC Action News. "UFO sighting over Philly?" October 8, 2008. (accessed September 2014) http://6abc.com/archive/6438701/

Advertiser. "Aliens leave ADF cold." 22 November 1996. 8.

Aimé Michel. *"The Truth About Flying Saucers" ("Mystérieux objects célestes")*. ed. Arthaud 1958.

Alberta Genweb. (accessed September 2014) http://www.rootsweb.ancestry.com/~abcamros/

Alberta's Francophone Heritage Infokit. (accessed September 2014) http://www.edukits.ca/francophone/en/elementary/infomania_text_french.html

Anderson Benedict. *Imagined Communities—Reflections on the Origins and Spread of Nationalism*. London: Verso 1983.

Arsenault Raymond. *Freedom Riders: 1961 and the Struggle for Racial Justice*. Oxford: Oxford University Press 2006.

Baghdjian Alice. "The truth is out there: U.K. X-files put online." *Times – Colonist* 14 August 2011. D8.

Barnett Antony. "The timebomb that threatens Britain." *The Observer*. Sunday 24 October 1999. (accessed September 2014) http://www.theguardian.com/uk/1999/oct/24/theobserver.uknews5

Bartholomew Robert E. "Ethnocentricity and the social construction of mass hysteria." *Culture, Medicine and Psychiatry*. Vol.14. Issue 4. 1990. 455-494

Basterfield Keith and M.A. Thalbourne. "Belief in and Alleged Experience of the Paranormal in Ostensible UFO Abductees."

Australian Journal of Parapsychology 2 (1) 2-18

— "Paranormal Aspects of the UFO Phenomenon: 1975-1999." *Australian Journal of Parapsychology* 1(1): 30-55

BBC News. "Brazil air force to record UFO sightings." 11 August 2010. (accessed September 2014) http://www.bbc.com/news/world-latin-america-10947856

— "1980: Government announces missile sites" *On This Day In History* (accessed September 2014) http://news.bbc.co.uk/onthisday/hi/dates/stories/june/17/newsid_2514000/2514879.stm

— "Files released on UFO sightings." (page last modified 14 May 2008) http://news.bbc.co.uk/2/hi/uk_news/7398108.stm

Berton Pierre. *1967, the Last Good Year*. Doubleday Canada; 1st Edition September 2, 1997.

Besser Linton. "Alien abduction? We'll probably never know." *Katherine Times*. 14 August 2011. (accessed September 2014) http://www.katherinetimes.com.au

Blechman Barry M. and Stephen S. Kaplan. *Force Without War*. Washington: Brookings Institution Press 1978.

Boitte Franck. "Belgian Ufology: What Future Developments Are to Be Expected after the Petit-Rechain Fiasco?" (accessed September 2014) http://www.cobeps.org/pdf/belgian_wave_130310.pdf

Bougard Michel and Lucien Clerebaut. "Chronique d'une vague." In *SOBEPS, Vague d'OVNI sur la Belgique: Un dossier exceptionnel*. p 51. Bruxelles: SOBEPS 1991.

Bray Arthur. *The UFO Connection*. Ottawa: Jupiter Publishing 1979.

Brennan Zoe. "What IS the truth about the Enfield Poltergeist? Amazing story of 11-year-old London girl who 'levitated' above her bed." *Daily Mirror* 28 October 2011. (accessed September 2014) http://www.dailymail.co.uk/news/article-2054842/Enfield-Poltergeist-The-amazing-story-11-year-old-North-London-girl-levitated-bed.html

Brovetto P. and V. Maxia. "Some conjectures about the mechanism of poltergeist phenomenon." *NeuroQuantology* 6, No. 2. 1-8.

Bryan C.D.B. *Close Encounters of the Fourth Kind: Alien abduction, UFOs, and the conference at M.I.T.* New York: Knopf 1995.

Budden A. *Electric UFOs: Fireballs, electromagnetics and abnormal states.* Darby, England: Diane Publishing 1998.

Budden Albert. *UFOs Psychic Close Encounters: The electromagnetic indictment.* London: Blandford, 1995.

CAELESTIA. "Famous Belgian UFO photo a hoax." (accessed September 2014) http://www.caelestia.be/article05ad.html

Cardoso Rodrigo. "A história oficial dos ÓVNIS no Brasil." *Istoé Independente,* 22 July 2009. (accessed September 2014) http://www. istoe.com.br/reportagens/11862_A+HISTORIA+OFICIAL+DOS+OV NIS+NO+BRASIL

Carlson Peter. "Alien Armada! 50 Years Ago, Unidentified Flying Objects From ..." *Washington Post.* 21 July. F01.

Cassirer Manfred. *Parapsychology and the UFO.* London: n.p. 1988.

C.E.F.O.R.A. (accessed September 2014) http://www.cefora.com.ar/ firmar_fichas.htm

Central Intelligence Agency. *"The Future of Eastern Europe – Key Judgements."* April 1990. vii.

Centre du patrimoine. "La chanson des Bois-Brûlés." (accessed September 2014) http://shsb.mb.ca/node/374

Clark J. "Interview with Jacques Vallée." In *Proceedings of the First International UFO Congress,* Curtis G Fuller ed. p. 405 New York: Warner, 1980.

Clark Jerome and Loren Coleman. *The Unidentified.* New York: Warner 1975. Reprinted in *The Unidentified & Creatures of the Outer Edge,* The Early Works of Jerome Clark and Loren Coleman, (San Antonio: Anomalist Books, 2006)

Clarke David. "New Light on Rendlesham" (accessed September 2014) http://drdavidclarke.co.uk/secret-files/secret-files-4/

Clas Svahn. "The Swedish Military UFO History." In *UFOs and*

Government: An Historical Inquiry. Michael Sword and Robert Powell eds. p. 371 San Antonio: Anomalist Books, 2012

Claudeir Covo. "Maio de 86 - A Mobilizaçao No Céu Brasileiro." *UFOLOGIA*, No. 14, Editora Trés, Sao Paulo, 1986.

COBEPS "Vague d'OVNI sur la Belgique 1989-1991," COBEPS (accessed September 2014) http://www.cobeps.org/fr/vague_belge.html

Collyns Dan. "Peru's UFO investigations office to be reopened," *The Guardian*, 27 October 2013. (accessed Sept 2014) http://www.theguardian.com/world/2013/oct/27/peru-ufo-investigations-office-reopening

Comisión de Estudio de Fenómenos Aeroespaciales, Fuerza Aérea Argentina. (accessed September 2014) http://www.fuerzaaerea.mil.ar/prensa/cefae.html

Comité de estudios de fenómenos aéreos anómalos C.E.F.A.A. (accessed September 14 2014) http://www.cefaa.gob.cl/web/quienessomos.html.

Corrales Scott. *Chupacabras and Other Mysteries*. Austin: Greenleaf Publications 1997.

Creighton G. "The Humanoids in Latin America," *Flying Saucer Review - Special Issue* October-November 1966. 30-46.

Creighton G. "The amazing case of Antonio Villas Boas." In *UFO Abductions: True cases of alien kidnapping*. pp. 51 -85. Scott Rogo ed. New York: Signet 1980.

Creston. The Alien Digest Vol. 4. (accessed September 2014) http://www.projectcamelot.org/Alien_Digest_Vol_4.pdf

Davies O. *The Haunted: A Social History of Ghosts*. London: Palgrave Macmillan 2009.

De Brouwer Wilfred. "Postface." In SOBEPS, *Vague d'OVNI sur la Belgique: Un dossier exceptionnel*. Bruxelles: SOBEPS. 491.

Dennett Michael. "A final interview with Milbourne Christopher." *Skeptical Inquirer* 9:2 (Winter 1984–85).

Devereux Paul. *Earthlights*. Wellingborough: Turnstone Press 1982.

Duff Michelle. "Defence wants UFOs off its radar." *The Dominion Post*. 31 March 2011. A7.

Easton James. "Rendlesham Revelations" *Fortean Times*. (accessed September 2014) http://www.forteantimes.com/features/articles/257/rendlesham_revelations.html

The Economist. "Television in Smoke-filled Rooms." 19 July 1952.

Edwards Rob. "US deployed nuclear weapons in the UK despite warning." *Science Direct*. (DOI: 10.1016/S0262-4079(07)61745-X) http://www.sciencedirect.com/science/article/pii/S026240790761745X

Eisenbud Jule. *Parapsychology and the Unconscious*. Berkeley: North Atlantic Book 1983.

El Pais. "Fuerza Aérea investiga foto de ovni tomada durante la caravana celeste." 21 July 2010. (accessed September 2014) http://historico.elpais.com.uy/100721/pciuda-503130/ciudades/Fuerza-Aerea-investiga-foto-de-ovni-tomada-durante-la-caravana-celeste/

Evans Hilary. *Visions, apparitions and alien visitors: A comparative study of the entity enigma*. London: Book Club Associates 1984.

Fanon Frantz. *"Black Skin, White Mask."* Trans. Charles L. Markmann. USA: Grove Press 1967.

Favre F. ed. *Les apparitions mystérieuses*. Paris: Tchou/Laffont 1978.

Feindt Carl. Water UFO.net. (accessed September 2014) http://www.waterufo.net

Ferryn Patrick. "Vidéofilms et photographies." In *SOBEPS, Vague d'OVNI sur la Belgique: Un dossier exceptionnel*, p. 397 Bruxelles: SOBEPS 1991.

Find Law.com. "LOVING v. VIRGINIA. 388 U.S. 1. 1967." (accessed September 2014) http://laws.findlaw.com/us/388/1.html

Fodor Nandor. *On the trail of the poltergeist*. New York: Citadel Press 1958.

Fondation René-Lévesque. "Projet de lettre adressée à Jean Lesage (2

août 1967).” (accessed September 2014) http://fondationrene-levesque.
org/documentation/ecrits-de-rene-levesque/textes/projet-de-lettre-
adressee-a-jean-lesage-2-aout-1967/

Forshufvud Ragnar. “UFO, ett fysykalist fenomen.” UFO-Sverige-
Aktuellt 1, No. 1. 1980.

Fort Charles. New Land. New York: Boni & Liveright 1923.

Fowler Raymond. The Andreasson Affair. Englewood Cliffs: Prentice-
Hall 1979.

Fox News.com. “Russian Navy Reveals Its Secret UFO Encounters.”
28 July 2009 (accessed September 2014) http://www.foxnews.com/
story/2009/07/28/russian-navy-reveals-its-secret-ufo-encounters/

Friedman Stanton T. and Kathleen Marden. Captured! The Betty and
Barney Hill UFO Experience. New Page Books 2007.

Fuerza Aérea del Perú. (accessed September 2014) http://www.dinae.
fap.mil.pe/

Fuerza Aérea Uruguaya. (accessed September 14 2014) http://www.
fau.mil.uy/cridovni.html

Fuller J. G. The Interrupted Journey. New York: Medallion. 1966.

Gates Charlie. “UFO papers to be made public.” The Press, 23 January
2010. (accessed September 2014) http://www.stuff.co.nz/the-press/
news/3255698/UFO-papers-to-be-made-public

Gilmor Daniel. Ed. Final Report of the Scientific Study of Unidentified
Flying Objects. New York: Bantam Books, 1969.

Girardet R. La crise militaire française 1945-1960: Aspects
sociologiques et idéologiques. Paris: Armand Colin 1964.

Global Security.org. “Orford Ness.” (accessed September 2014) http://
www.globalsecurity.org/wmd/world/uk/orford_ness.htm

Greenwood Barry J. and Bill Fawcett. The UFO Cover-up. New York:
Touchstone, 1990.

Haines Gerald K. “CIA’s Role in the Study of UFOs, 1947-90.”
(accessed September 2014) https://www.cia.gov/library/center-for-the-

study-of-intelligence/csi-publications/csi-studies/studies/97unclass/ufo.html

Hall Richard H. "Alien Invasion of Human Fantasy? The 1966-67 UFO wave." Washington: Fund for UFO Research 2004.

— "Hill Radar-UFO Connection Weak." *MUFON UFO Journal* No.140.

— 1967: The Overlooked UFO Wave and The Colorado Project." *MUFON 1978 UFO Symposium Proceedings.* 51-74

— and Karl T. Pflock. "Book review." Journal of Scientific Exploration. (accessed September 2014) http://www.scientificexploration.org/journal/reviews/reviews_18_4_pflock_2.pdf

Hansen George P. *The Trickster and the Paranormal.* Philadelphia: Xlibris 2001.

Harvey-Wilson Simon. "Shamanism and Alien Abductions: A Comparative Study." *Australian Journal of Parapsychology* 2 (1): 103-116.

Healy Alison. "Irish UFOs blast into the light after 37 years in twilight zone." *The Irish Times* 20 September 2007 (accessed September 2014) http://www.ireland.com/newspaper/frontpage/2007/0920/1190238990654.html

Heath Pamela Rae. *The PK Zone: A cross-cultural review of psychokinesis.* Lincoln: iUniverse, 2003.

Heazell P. *Most Secret: The Hidden history of Orford Ness.* Stroud: The History Press 2010.

Henningsen Ole."Exciting release of Air Force UFO archives." *Scandinavian UFO Information* (SUFOI). 28 January 2009. (accessed September 2014) http://www.sufoi.dk/english/flyufo-uk.php

Hynek J. Allen. *The Hynek Report.* New York: Dell Book, 1977.

Iliff Laurence. "We are not alone,' military pilot says." *The Gazette*, 26 July 2004. A19.

International Consciousness Research Laboratories. (accessed September 2014) http://www.icrl.org/

Jacobs D.M. "The UFO experience: A normal correlate of human brain function." In *UFOs and abductions: Challenging the borders of knowledge*. pp. 262-302. Lawrence: University Press of Kansas, 2000.

Jung C.G. *Flying Saucers* Trans by R.F.C Hull. New York: MJF 1978.

— *Man and his symbols*, New York: Dell. 1964.

Kean Leslie. *UFOS, Generals, Pilots, and Government Records*. New York: Three Rivers Press, 2010.

Keel John. "Is the EM effect a myth?" *Flying Saucer Review* 14, No. 6 1968.

— "North America 1966: Development of a Great Wave." *Flying Saucer Review*, Vol. 13 (2) Mar.-Apr. 1967.

— "The people problem." In *Phenomenon: Forty years of flying saucers*. Spencer J. and H. Evans eds. pp. 186-198 New York: Avon Books, 1988.

Keul Alexander. "Ball lightning reports." *Naturwissenschaften* (68) 1981. 134-136.

— and Ken Phillips, (1986) 'The unidentified witness." *Journal of Transient Aerial Phenomena*. (4). 43-44.

Keyhoe Donald E. *Flying Saucers from Outer Space*. New York: Holt, 1953.

Kirby D. "UFOs: Guatemala gripped by ET fever." *The Ottawa Citizen*. 5 March 1989. E4.

Kottmeyer Martin. "UFO Flaps." *The Anomalist* 3. 1995-1996. 64-89.

La Capital. "Piden desclasificar datos oficiales sobre ovnis." 14 September 201 (accessed Sept 2014) http://www.lacapital.com.ar/la-ciudad/Piden-desclasificar-datos-oficiales-sobre-ovnis--20130914-0017.html

Lagarde Ferdinand. *Flying Saucer Review*. 14, No. 6. 1968.

— *Mystérieuses soucoupes volantes*. Paris: Étapes, 1973.

Ledger Don and Chris Styles. *Dark Object: The world's only government documented UFO crash.* New York: Dell 2001.

Leslie D and G. Adamski. *Flying Saucers Have Landed.* London: Thomas Werner Laurie 1953.

Library and Archives Canada. "History of Industry in Hamilton." (accessed September 2014) http://epe.lac-bac.gc.ca/100/205/301/ic/ cdc/industrial/history.htm.

— "Industrial Hamilton: a trail to the future, Stelco, Incorporated The Steel Company of Canada." (accessed September 2014) http://epe. lac-bac.gc.ca/100/205/301/ic/cdc/industrial/stelcomain.htm

— "Timeline of Hamilton Industry." (accessed September 2014) http:// epe.lac-bac.gc.ca/100/205/301/ic/cdc/industrial/timeline1979.htm

— Canada's UFOs: The Search for the Unknown. (accessed September 2014) http://www.collectionscanada.gc.ca/ufo/002029- 2501-e.html

— Canada's UFOs: The Search for the Unknown." (accessed September 2014) http://www.collectionscanada.gc.ca/ufo/002029- 2501-e.html

Lorenzen Coral. *Flying Saucers: The startling evidence of the invasion from outer space.* New York: Signet 1962.

Magonia Magazine Archive. (accessed September 2014) http:// magonia.haaan.com/

Magor John. "1967 Canadian UFO Wave: The Year We Were Invaded Without Knowing It." UFO Evidence. (accessed September 2014) http://www.ufoevidence.org/documents/doc683.htm

McNally Richard J. "Explaining "memories" of space alien abduction and past lives: An experimental psychopathology approach." *Journal of Experimental Psychopathology* 3 (1) 2-16.

Meessen Auguste. "La détection radar." In SOBEPS, *Vague d'OVNI sur la Belgique: Un dossier exceptionnel.* pp. 364-365 Bruxelles:SOBEPS 1991b.

— "Les observations décisives du 29 novembre 1989." In *SOBEPS, Vague d'OVNI sur la Belgique: Un dossier exceptionnel.* P. 25

Bruxelles: SOBEPS 1991a

Military.net. NIE 11-8/1-61 – "Strength and Deployment of Soviet Long Range Ballistic Missile Forces." 21 September 1961 (accessed December 22, 2008) http://www.milnet.com/cia/nies/1961.htm

Ministério da Defesa. (accessed September 2014) http://www.defesa. gov.br/index.php/ultimas-noticias/8651-ministerio-da-defesa-recebe-ufologos-para-tratar-de-documentos-sobre-ovnis

National Archives of Australia. Unidentified flying objects UFOs. (accessed September 2014) http://www.naa.gov.au/collection/a-z/ufos. aspx

The National Investigations Committee on Aerial Phenomena NICAP (accessed September 2014) http://www.nicap.org/

National Post "Resources cited as Britain closes unit that investigates UFO sightings." 5 December 2009. A28.

NATO Review. Vol. 38. No. 2 April 1990. 16 – 23.

Nickell Joe. *The Science of Ghosts: Searching for Spirits of the Dead.* Amherst: Prometheus Books 2012.

Ouellet E. "Extending von Lucadou's Model of Pragmatic Information to UFOs: A case study of the 1952 Washington DC UFO Wave." *Australian Journal of Parapsychology, 11* (2), 116-137.

— "Social Psi: A Framework for Understanding Large Scale Anomalies" *EdgeScience 18* (June 2014). 5-11.

— "Social psi and parasociology." *Australian Journal of Parapsychology. 11* (1) 73-88.

Ovni-Suisse.ch. "L'armée française de l'air peut prendre en chasse les soucoupes volantes." (accessed September 2014) http://www.ovni-suisse.ch/fr/documentations/coupures-presse/l-armee-francaise-de-l-air-peut-prendre-en-chasse-les-soucoupes-volantes-713

Owen I. M. and M Sparrow. "*Conjuring up Philip: An adventure in psychokinesis.*" Toronto Canada: Harper & Row 1976.

Partain Keith L. *Psi in the Sky: A new approach to UFO and psi phenomena*. Philadelphia: Xlibris 2001.

Patrimonium, Histoire de Fexhe et Slins. "Histoire du Radar." (accessed September 2014) http://fexhe-slins-patrimonium.weebly. com/radar-de-glons.html

Peel Bruce. "FALCON PIERRE." In Dictionary of Canadian Biography, vol. 10. University of Toronto/Université Laval, 2003. (accessed September 18, 2014) http://www.biographi.ca/en/bio/falcon_ pierre_10E.html

Persinger M. and R. A Cameron. "Are earth faults at fault in some poltergeist-like episodes?" *Journal of the American Society for Psychical Research* 80 (1986): 49-73.

—"ELF field mediation in spontaneous PSI events: direct information transfer or conditioned elicitation?" *Psychoenergetic Systems* 3 (1979): 155-169.

— "Geophysical models for parapsychological experiences" *Psychoenergetic Systems* 1 (1975): 63-74.

— and S. A. Koren. "Predicting the characteristics of haunts from geomagnetic factors and brain sensitivity: Evidence from field and experimental studies." In *Hauntings and poltergeists: Multidisciplinary perspectives*. Houran J and Lange R pp 179-194. Jefferson: McFarland & Company 2001.

— and G.F Lafrenière. *Space-time Transients and Unusual Events*. Chicago: Nelson-Hall, 1977.

— "Spontaneous telepathic experiences from Phantasms of the Living and Low Global Geomagnetic Activity" *Journal of the American Society for Psychical Research* 81 (1987) 23-36.

— "The tectonic strain theory as an explanation for UFO phenomena: A nontechnical review of the research, 1970-1990." *Journal of UFO Studies* 2 (1990) 105-137.

Pickles D. "The seven-year struggle in Algeria: Retrospect and prospect." *The World Today*, 17 (11) 479-489.

Playfair Guy Lyon. *This House is Haunted: the True Story of a Poltergeist*. London: Stein & Day, 1980.

Pope Nick. *Open Skies, Closed Minds*. London: Overlook Press, 1999.

Primary Metals. "The Steel Making Industry." (accessed September 2014) http://www.istc.illinois.edu/info/library_docs/manuals/primmetals/chapter2.htm

Princeton Engineering Anomalies Research. (accessed September 2014) http://www.princeton.edu/~pear/

Project 1947. "Official UFO Study Programs in Foreign Countries."(accessed September 2014) http://www.project1947.com/shg/condon/s5chap03.html.

Radin Dean. *Entangled minds: Extrasensory experiences in a quantum reality*. New York: Paraview 2006.

Randle Kevin. *Invasion Washington: UFOs over the Capitol*. New York: HarperCollins 2001.

Randles Jenny. *Alien Contacts: The first fifty years*. New York: Barnes & Noble Books 1997.

— "View from Britain," *MUFON UFO Journal No. 432* April 2004 18-19.

— *UFO Reality: A Critical Look at the Physical Evidence*. London: R. Hale, 1983.

Rayl A.J.S. "Into The Night" Omni Project: Open Book (accessed September 2014) http://web.archive.org/web/19970607031756/www.omnimag.com/open_book/bent11.html

Redfern Nick. *Contactees: A History of Alien-Human Interaction*. Pompton Plains NJ: Career Press 2009.

— *The F.B.I. Files: The FBI's UFO top secrets exposed*. London: Pocket Books 1998.

Ridpath Ian. "Interview With J. Allen Hynek." *Nature*. Vol. 251. October 1975.

— Rendlesham Forest. (accessed September 2014) http://www.ianridpath.com/ufo/rendlesham.htm

Rogo Scott. *The Haunted Universe*. San Antonio: Anomalist 2006.

— Minds and motion: The riddle of psychokinesis. New York: Taplinger Publishing 1978.

Rojcewicz Peter M. "The 'Men in Black' experience and tradition: Analogues with the traditional devil hypothesis." *Journal of American Folklore* 100 (396): 148-160.

Roll William G. "Poltergeists, Electromagnetism and Consciousness." *Journal of Scientific Exploration* 17. 1. 75–86.

— and M.A. Persinger. "Poltergeists and hauntings." In *Hauntings and poltergeists: Multidisciplinary perspectives*. Houran J and Lange R pp 123-163. Jefferson: McFarland & Company 2001.

—. *The Poltergeist*. New York: Paraview 1972.

Rosales Albert S. "Humanoid Sighting Reports & Journal of Humanoid Studies." (accessed September 2014) http://www.ufoinfo.com/humanoid/humanoid1967.shtml.

Rouse Wayne R. and John G. McCutcheon."The effect of the regional wind on air pollution in Hamilton, Ontario." *Canadian Geographer* 14 (4): 271-285.

Roussel Robert. "OVNI, la fin du secret." Belfond 1978 (accessed September 2014). http://www.rhedae-magazine.com/OVNI-1976-la-position-officielle-de-l-armee-de-l-air-par-le-responsable-de-l-etude-du-phenomene_a716.html

Rutkowski Chris and Geoff Dittman. "The Prime Minister and the UFO." In *The Canadian UFO Report: the Best Cases Revealed*, pp 212-218 Dundurn Press, 2006.

Schaut G.B and M. A Persinger."Subjective telepathic experiences, geomagnetic activity and the ELF hypothesis: Part I. Data analyses." *PSI Research*. 4 No. 1 (1985) 4-20.

Schmitt Jean-Claude. *"Ghosts in the Middle Ages: The Living and the Dead in Medieval Society."* Chicago: University of Chicago Press 1999.

Schrecker Ellen. *The Age of McCarthyism*. New York: Palgrave, 2002.

Schwarz Berthold. *UFO Dynamics: Psychiatric and psychic aspects of the UFO syndrome*. Moore Haven: Rainbow Books 1988.

Sheldrake Rupert. "Morphic Fields and Morphic Resonance." *Noetic Now*. (accessed September 2014) http://www.noetic.org/noetic/issue-four-november-2010/morphic-fields-and-morphic-resonance/

Simon Benjamin. "Introduction." In *The Interrupted Journey*, John Fuller p.5 New York: Berkeley Publishing.

Spanos N. P. "Close encounters: An examination of UFO experiences." *Journal of Abnormal Psychology*. (102) 624-632.

Spencer John and A. Spencer. *The Poltergeist Phenomenon*. London: Headline, 1997.

Spurgeon David. "U of T aerospace institute plans full-scale study of UFOs." The Globe and Mail. September 20 1967. 1.

Steiger Brad. *Project Blue Book*. Ballantine Books 1976.

Stelco Research Blog. "Stelco R & D." (accessed September 2014) http://stelcoresearch.blogspot.com/2008/09/opening-of-stelco-research-centre.html

Strand Erling P. Project Hessdalen. (accessed September 2014) http://www.hessdalen.org/

Sudbury Star. Sudbury in the 1960s. (accessed September 2014) http://www.thesudburystar.com/ArticleDisplay.aspx?archive=true&e=1270773

Suffolk Constabulary website. (accessed September 2014) http://www.suffolk.police.uk/aboutus/yourrighttoinformation/freedomofinformation/publicationscheme/idoc.ashx?docid=8639184b-b8fe-40ed-9b8c-932bd724e1c4&version=-1

Tennyson Rod. "The UTIAS UFO Project." *The UTIAS Newsletter* 2009 (2) 3.

Tokarz Harry. "UFO Witnesses, Public Property?" MUFOB new series 11. Summer 1978.

UFO Evidence. "Lambrechts Report." (accessed September 2014) http://www.ufoevidence.org/documents/doc408.htm

— "Report concerning the observation of UFOs in the night from

March 30 to March 31, 1990." (accessed September 2014) http://www.ufoevidence.org/documents/doc408.htm

— Shag Harbour. (accessed September 2014) http://www.ufoevidence.org/Cases/CaseSubarticle.asp?ID=179

UFO Joe. Canadian X-Files. (accessed September 2014) http://ufo-joe.tripod.com

UK Parliament. "German Unification." (accessed September 2014) http://hansard.millbanksystems.com/commons/1990/apr/03/german-unification

United Kingdom. The Redfern Inquiry: into human tissue analysis in UK nuclear facilities, Volume 1: Report, United Kingdom, 16 November 2010. (accessed September 2014) https://www.gov.uk/government/uploads/system/uploads/attachment_data/file/229155/0571_i.pdf

—, *Unidentified Aerial Phenomena (UAP) in the UK Air Defence Region.* London: Ministry of Defence 2000.

 United States National Archive. *"Unidentified Flying Objects -Project BLUE BOOK."* (accessed Sept 2014) http://www.archives.gov/foia/ufos.html

Vallée Jacques. *The Invisible College: What UFO Scientists Know about the Nature of Alien Influences on the Human Race.* Penguin, 1977; Anomalist Books, 2014.

— *Messengers of Deception: UFO contacts and cults.* Berkeley: And/Or Press 1979.

— *Passport to Magonia: From folklore to flying saucers.* Chicago, IL: Regnery 1969

— *UFOs: The Psychic Solution.* St. Albans.: Panther, 1977.

Van De Castlea R. L. "The Facilitation of ESP through Hypnosis." *American Journal of Clinical Hypnosis.* Vol 12, (1) 1969. 37-56.

Van Tassel G. W. *I Rode a Flying Saucer!* Los Angeles: New Age Publishing 1952.

Viéroudy Pierre. *Ces ovnis qui annoncent le surhomme*. Paris: Tchou 1977.

Von Lucadou Walter. "The exo-endo-perspective of nonlocality in psycho-physical systems." *Cases, International Journal of Computing Anticipatory Systems* 2. 1998. 169– 185.

— "The Model of Pragmatic Information MPI." *European Journal of Parapsychology* 11. 1995. 58–75.

— and F. Zahradnik. "Predictions of the Model of Pragmatic Information about RSPK." *Proceedings of the Parapsychological Association Convention* 2004.

— H. Römer, and H. Walach. "Synchronistic phenomena as entanglement correlations in generalized quantum theory." *Journal of Consciousness Studies*, 14 (4) 2007. 50–74.

Washington: Department of the Air Force. "United States, Air *Force Regulation No.* 200-2, 1954.

World Nuclear Association. Uranium in Canada. (accessed September 2014) http://www.worldnuclear.org/info/inf49.html

Wuttunee Stephane. "Blossom Goodchild's Predicted Mass UFO Sighting: Will it Force Disclosure to Occur?" UFO Digest. (accessed September 2014) http://www.ufodigest.com/news/0908/blossom.html

Youtube. "UFOs over Philly during Bruce Springsteen/Obama concert." uploaded on 6 Oct 2008 by user juno2070. (accessed September 2014) https://www.youtube.com/watch?v=Qi5Wmby9dSE

Zervoudakis A. "A case of successful pacification." In *France and the Algerian War: Strategy, operations and diploma*. eds. M. Alexander & J. F. V. Keiger. pp. 54-64. London: Frank Cass 2002.

Index

About the Author

Eric Ouellet is a professor of military sociology with the Royal Military College of Canada, and he is Head of the Department of Defence Studies at the Canadian Forces College in Toronto. He teaches middle and senior level military officers posted to advanced professional development studies. As part of his work, he is also engaged in conducting scholarly research and publishing, and has been involved in a number of applied research projects for the North Atlantic Treaty Organization, and for Defence Research and Development Canada. He has published on various topics such as military leadership, command and control, military planning, irregular warfare and terrorism, institutional analysis of military organizations, and strategic studies.

He is a professional member of the Parapsychological Association (PA), the only formally recognized scholarly society in the field of parapsychology, and he is the PA's liaison officer for Canada. He has written a number of articles on parapsychological topics in publications like the *Australian Journal of Parapsychology*, *Bulletin Métapsychique*, *EdgeScience*, and *Paranthropology*. His research is focussed on developing a better understanding of paranormal phenomena's role in social dynamics with a particular emphasis on the UFO phenomenon. He is also collaborating with a Canadian paranormal research organization, Paranormal Studies Investigations Canada (PSICAN).

Eric Ouellet studied political science at Université Laval, in Quebec City, where he completed a Baccalaureate and a Master's degree. He graduated with a Ph.D. in sociology from York University, in Toronto. He was born in Quebec City, Canada, and moved to Toronto in 1992.

Printed in the USA
CPSIA information can be obtained
at www.ICGtesting.com
LVHW021058010224
770613LV00008B/375